Breaking the Stained-glass Ceiling

Breaking the Stained-glass Ceiling
A Critical Analysis of Women in Ministry in the Black Church

Sunday School Publishing Board
Nashville, Tennessee

Copyright © 2025 by the Sunday School Publishing Board. All rights reserved.

No part of this work may be reproduced or transmitted in any form, by any means, electronic or mechanical, including photocopying, recording, or by any information storage or retrieval system without prior written permission from the publisher. Send permission requests to the Sunday School Publishing Board, P. O. Box 70990, Nashville, Tennessee 37207-0990; or e-mail to customercare@sspbnbc.com.

Scripture marked KJV is taken from the King James Version of the Holy Bible. Scripture marked NIV is taken from the Holy Bible, New International Version®, NIV® Copyright ©1973, 1978, 1984, 2011 by Biblica, Inc.® Used by permission. All rights reserved worldwide. Scripture marked NRSVUE is taken from the New Revised Standard Version, Updated Edition. Copyright © 2021 National Council of Churches of Christ in the United States of America. Used by permission. All rights reserved worldwide.

A Notice on Web sites: Any Web sites listed in this book were reviewed and found to be active and appropriate at the time this resource was developed. Unfortunately, these things change constantly, so just be aware of this fact in case any of them have since gone defunct.

ISBN: 978-1-957621-76-0

Printed in the United States of America.

This work is lovingly dedicated to my wife of more than twenty years, Rev. Shevalle T. Kimber—my covenant partner in life, in love, and in ministry. Together we have walked through seasons of growth, challenge, and divine purpose—hand in hand and heart to heart. She has been the steady rhythm of our home and the spiritual heartbeat of our family: a devoted mother to our children, a wise counselor, and a woman whose strong faith remains constant. Shevalle is accomplished in her own right as co-pastor, chaplain, spiritual counselor, author, and co-host of the Woman to Woman segment on WTNH News 8. After receiving her call to ministry following our union in marriage, she went on to earn a Bachelor of Arts degree from American Baptist College in Nashville, Tennessee, and a Master of Divinity degree from Yale Divinity School in New Haven, Connecticut. Through her calling, I came to understand more deeply the sacred power and prophetic voice of women in ministry. Her steadfast faith, devotion to God's work, and pursuit of excellence continue to inspire me every day. Her prayers have sustained my journey, her wisdom has sharpened my purpose, and her love remains a wellspring of grace and encouragement. I am profoundly grateful for the woman she is and the light she continues to shine.

This dedication also extends to all women in ministry—past, present, and future—whose faith, courage, and gifts enrich the body of Christ and advance the Gospel of Jesus Christ.

To the beloved congregation I have had the honor of serving for the past forty years at First Calvary Baptist Church of New Haven, Connecticut, thank you. To New Hope Baptist Church of Bridgeport, Connecticut, the Connecticut State Missionary Baptist Convention, and the National Baptist Convention, USA, Inc.—thank you for your steadfast labor in the vineyard and for standing with us as co-laborers in the kingdom of God.

Table of Contents

Foreword ix
Preface xiii
Acknowledgments xv
Introduction 1

Chapter 1
Black Women: The Foundation of the Black Church 3
    Black Woman as Mother in the Community 14
    Black Women as Leaders of the Church 16

Chapter 2
Black Women: Willing Workers 21
    Baptist 21
    Methodist 23
    Jarena Lee and Zilpha Elaw 27
    Prathia Hall 32
    Barbara Harris 37

Chapter 3
From History to Herstory:
Black Women in Contemporary Ministry 41
    Call 42
    Challenges 45
    Joys 52

Chapter 4
Future Role of Women in Ministry as a Catalyst for the Black Church Survival 59
    Being Led by the Spirit 59
    The Responsibility of Men 64
    The Agency of Women 73

CHAPTER 5
Bridging the Gap between Legacy and Destiny (Conclusion) 79

Works Cited 83

About the Author 87

Foreword

According to *The State of the Clergy Woman in the U.S.* (2018), women comprise 50 to 75 percent of church membership. They fill the choir stands and pews, fund ministries, and nurture the next generation of believers. Yet, they hold only 10 percent of leadership roles and account for less than 1 percent of senior pastor positions. This disparity is not merely an oversight—it is a theological crisis that raises urgent questions: Can women be licensed to preach if they have demonstrated a divine call to ministry? Can they be ordained after a thorough examination of their Christian experience, call, and doctrine? Can they be appointed as pastors after completing rigorous seminary education and pastoral training? These questions lie at the center of ongoing debates in African American Baptist communities, intensified by the recent Southern Baptist Convention's decision to exclude women from pastoral roles. To deny women full access to ministerial and leadership roles is not only unjust—it is un-Christlike. It reflects the same oppressive spirit that once sought to keep an entire people in bondage and still marginalizes Black women in society and the church.

Biblical scholarship affirms that the apostle Paul's—not Jesus'—admonitions in 1 Corinthians 14:34-35 and 1 Timothy 2:11-12 must be read in their historical and cultural contexts, rather than as universal prohibitions against women in ministry. These passages addressed specific challenges in the early church, including maintaining order and curbing disruptions during worship. Taken as timeless commands, they would imply that women should withhold their time, gifts, talents, and treasure—a reality that would be catastrophic for the Black church. Similarly, focusing solely on Paul's requirement that a pastor be *"the husband of one wife"* (1 Timothy 3:2, KJV) while neglecting other qualifications—being *"above reproach,"* *"self-controlled,"* and *"able to teach"* (NIV)—is a narrow reading, especially since masculine language was often used exclusively in that culture. Addressing a woman today, Paul might well have said, *"the wife of one husband."*

Throughout the history of the Black church, one truth has remained constant: Black women have been its foundation. They prayed in it, built it, funded it, sang it into revival, and carried the weight of its mission on their shoulders. From the era of slavery to the present day, they have preached, organized, and led—while confronting racial injustice—as living proof that *"your sons and your daughters shall prophesy"* (Acts 2:17b, KJV). Their ministries testify that the Spirit of God does not discriminate in calling, gifting, or empowering. However, within the National Baptist Convention, USA, Inc., where women are the majority of delegates and members of affiliated churches, there has never been a dedicated space for them to minister with the same recognition and opportunities as men. Past Convention leadership has not only refrained from publicly affirming women in ministry but has, in some cases, actively sought to suppress them. That is why Dr. Kimber's work is both timely and timeless. *Breaking the Stained-glass Ceiling: A Critical Analysis of Women in Ministry in the Black Church* began as his master's thesis at Yale Divinity School in 2018. Even then, it was a courageous and necessary intervention in the conversation about gender, race, power, and the Black church. Today, it remains both a scholarly contribution and a prophetic challenge.

Dr. Kimber does not simply call for change—he models it. In his first term as President of the NBCUSAI, which began in September 2024, he appointed women ministers and pastors to his cabinet, placed them in leadership roles, invited them to preach and pray in national worship services, and—in a historic move—appointed the first woman to chair the Board of Directors of the Sunday School Publishing Board. He has engaged women in denominational work well beyond the traditional Women's and Music Auxiliaries—more than any president in the history of the NBCUSAI. His commitment is equally evident in his home. Married to Rev. Shevalle T. Kimber, a powerful preacher who proclaims the Gospel nationwide, he embodies with her the conviction that God's call to service transcends gender and that the church is strongest when all of God's gifts are fully embraced.

If the twenty-first-century Black church is to both survive and thrive in a post-COVID-19 era, it must confront and dismantle the systemic barriers that continue to silence and marginalize half of its body. Without women, there is no Black church; and without the full affirmation of women in ministry, there can be no complete or credible witness to the Gospel. Scripture consistently affirms that in Christ, all believers are gifted, called, and equipped to serve for the edification of the whole body. To that end, the church must reclaim the inclusive and Spirit-led mission of the early Christian community. The mandate of the Great Commission (see Matthew 28:18-20) is clear: the evangelization, baptism, and teaching of all people. Likewise, our congregations are called to embody the life of the early *ekklesia*, birthed at Pentecost (see Acts 2), where the Holy Spirit descended not selectively, but universally—empowering sons and daughters, young and old alike, to prophesy, preach, and bear witness *"unto the uttermost part of the earth"* (Acts 1:8b). Such a return to our foundational identity is not innovation—it is restoration.

This book challenges the educable, the open-minded, and even the comfortable—those willing to confront the contradiction between the liberating Gospel proclaimed and the exclusionary practices perpetuated in many churches. Each chapter invites readers to envision a church where gender is no barrier to calling, where leadership is affirmed by both the Spirit and the community, and where the gifts of women are embraced as indispensable to the health and future of the Black church. Ultimately, this work is more than history—it is a theological reckoning, a pastoral challenge, and a prophetic summons. It calls the church to rise above inherited biases, to align its practice with the inclusive mission of Christ, and to bear witness to the truth that the body of Christ is incomplete until every God-given gift is welcomed, affirmed, and set free to serve its purpose.

Dr. Debbie A. Strickling-Bullock
Executive Pastor, Canaan Baptist Church of Delaware
Chair, Board of Directors, Sunday School Publishing Board
National Baptist Convention, USA, Inc.

Preface

This book was born out of both observation and conviction. For decades, I have served the Black church as a preacher, pastor, organizer, advocate, and leader within the National Baptist Convention, USA, Inc., and I have witnessed firsthand the indispensable contributions of Black women to its vitality. I have also witnessed, with equal clarity, the barriers that too often hinder them from serving in the fullness of their calling.

From the earliest days of my ministry in Alabama, my faith and formation have been shaped by the prayers, service, and spiritual leadership of women in the church. They were the teachers of my first Sunday School classes, the ushers who welcomed me into worship, the intercessors who covered me in prayer through seasons of trial, and the visionaries who advanced ministries when others hesitated. I also observed how many of these women were denied opportunities to lead from the pulpit or to shape theological discourse, even as they exercised remarkable leadership in practice. This disconnect between the Gospel's liberating message and the church's restrictive practices is not a new phenomenon. It is woven into the complex history of the Black church—an institution that has been both a sanctuary of justice and, at times, a site of exclusion. This tension compelled me to engage, through careful research and honest reflection, the historical, theological, and sociological realities that have defined and often constrained the role of women in ministry in the Black church context.

Breaking the Stained-glass Ceiling: A Critical Analysis of Women in Ministry in the Black Church began as my Master's Thesis at Yale Divinity School in 2018. My aim, then as now, was not merely to catalog injustices but to provide a critical framework for understanding them and, more importantly, to challenge us toward reform. This work examines the historical legacy of Black women in ministry, the cultural and doctrinal debates that have influenced their inclusion or exclusion in the Black church, and the contemporary realities they confront. It draws upon the stories of pioneering women whose courage broke through centuries-old barriers, as well as the voices of those still navigating these struggles in the twenty-first century.

While Scripture records the calling of men, nowhere does it declare that God called only men, nor does it imply that He would not call women. The sovereign God, who created both male and female in His image, affirms distinction without limitation and diversity without hierarchy. God's call arises from divine sovereignty, not human custom or cultural constraint. Throughout salvation history, God has used women as prophetic voices and spiritual leaders bearing witness that divine vocation extends beyond gender. When the church fails to recognize and empower all whom God has called, it diminishes its witness and resists the Spirit, who equips both sons and daughters to prophesy (see Joel 2:28; Acts 2:17).

As the nineteenth President of the National Baptist Convention, USA, Inc., my mission is to move our Convention from conversation to conviction, putting our belief into action. I have appointed women in ministry, including pastors, to my cabinet, placed them in leadership roles, and opened national platforms for them to preach, teach, and lead. These decisions are not symbolic; they are scriptural and reflect my conviction that what God ordains, the church must never restrain. Therefore, my prayer is that this book will serve as both a mirror and a roadmap so that we may see the inequities we have tolerated or perpetuated and chart a future where not only is the stained-glass ceiling shattered, but also the brick wall of resistance dismantled and the gifts of women are recognized and utilized as essential to the mission of the church. May this work inspire preachers, pastors, lay leaders, and congregations to reflect deeply, act courageously, and stand faithfully with the women who have stood so faithfully for the church.

Dr. Boise Kimber, President
National Baptist Convention, USA, Inc.

Acknowledgments

I extend my deepest gratitude to all who have contributed to the development of this work—to the staff and management of Townsend Press and the Sunday School Publishing Board of the National Baptist Convention, USA, Inc., for providing the platform, resources, and encouragement to bring this vision to life. I also honor Dr. Herron K. Gaston, Vincent E. Stokes, and those who have paved the way—trailblazers, mentors, and advocates—whose sacrifices, courage, and faith have made it possible to advance this vision for a more inclusive and equitable church. This work stands as a testament to their legacy. Finally, to every voice, prayer, and act of encouragement that has sustained me on this journey, thank you. Your belief in this mission continues to fuel my commitment to building a church and a convention that fully embrace the gifts and callings of all God's people.

Introduction

This biblical witness is clear: The mission of the church is incomplete without the full participation of women. Throughout the Gospels, Jesus affirmed women as vital to His mission—engaging the Samaritan woman in theological dialogue (see John 4:7-26), commending Mary of Bethany for choosing to learn at His feet (see Luke 10:38-42), and commissioning Mary Magdalene as the first witness of His resurrection (see John 20:16-18). In Acts 1:14, women are noted among those who prayed and prepared for the coming of the Holy Spirit. At Pentecost (see Acts 2), both men and women were filled with and empowered to proclaim the Gospel. To embrace their gifts is to follow the example of Christ, align with the leading of the Spirit, and live out the justice, equality, and love that are central to the Gospel. Only then can the church truly embody the Great Commission—evangelizing, baptizing, and teaching all nations with the full strength of the whole body of Christ.

Just as in biblical times, Black women have significantly shaped the modern Black church, both in visible and unseen ways. They have preached from pulpits, served in leadership, mobilized communities, and sustained ministries through prayer, vision, action, and financial support. While their influence is undeniable, their stories are too often underrepresented in the church's recorded history. This work examines those stories—past and present—while looking ahead to what the church can become when it fully embraces the leadership of women in ministry.

Chapter 1, "Black Women: The Foundation of the Black Church," traces how women established the moral and spiritual framework that has sustained Black congregations for generations. It considers their roles as cultural preservers, faith transmitters, and decision makers in community life, as well as their leadership within congregations—whether publicly acknowledged or exercised behind the scenes.

Chapter 2, "Black Women: Willing Workers," focuses on women whose service extended across denominational lines, with particular attention to the Baptist and Methodist traditions. It highlights the extraordinary ministries of Jarena Lee, Zilpha Elaw, Prathia Hall, and Barbara Harris, exploring how each made distinct contributions to the Gospel and challenged prevailing limitations on women in leadership.

Chapter 3, "From History to Herstory: Black Women in Contemporary Ministry," shifts to the present day, drawing from firsthand accounts of women currently serving in ministry. It examines the ways that they discern their calling, the barriers they continue to navigate, and the fulfillment they find in service. This chapter also illustrates how the past continues to influence the present, even as new opportunities arise.

Chapter 4, "The Future Role of Women in Ministry as a Catalyst for the Black Church Survival," offers a forward-looking perspective. It argues that the church's long-term health depends on the intentional inclusion of women at every level of leadership. The discussion addresses Spirit-led discernment, the shared responsibility of men and women in advancing equity, and the creation of structures that empower women to lead with authority and vision.

Chapter 5, "Bridging the Gap between Legacy and Destiny (Conclusion)," explores the future trajectory of women in ministry and argues that their presence is not simply beneficial but essential for the continued vitality of the Black church. This chapter outlines how the Spirit empowers women for leadership, examines the responsibility of men in dismantling oppressive systems, and highlights the agency and innovation that women bring to ministry. By placing women at the center of ecclesial survival, the chapter challenges the church to reconsider old paradigms and embrace a more equitable and Spirit-led future.

Together, these chapters present a layered view of the contributions, challenges, and potential of Black women in the Black church. The goal is not only to document history but also to shape the future, one in which no calling is diminished because of gender and every gift is welcomed for the good of the whole body.

Chapter 1

Black Women: The Foundation of the Black Church

In the tapestry of Christendom there are a myriad of religious experiences. From Gregorian Chants of the Roman Catholic Church to the Negro Spirituals of the Black church in America, Christianity continues to be a melting pot of liturgy and culture. The history of the Christian church has been told by the desert fathers and mothers, upheld by the tradition of ecclesiastical scholarship, and strengthened through the vanguards of the faith over two millennia.

The Christian church has grown from house churches that met in secret, to neighborhood churches where people gather as a community in one central location, to cathedrals which serve as national churches for a nation looking to ecclesiastical leaders for moral direction and focus. The hope for all churches is to share the liberating love of the Lord and make an impact through a common experience.

The history of the Christian church is both compelling and conflicting in the lives of believers. It was the church that began a culture of anti-intellectualism when science contradicted sacrament and Galileo pushed back against a geocentric view of the earth in favor of a heliocentric perspective.

The Scripture stated that the earth was firmly planted and established and could not be moved (see 1 Chronicles 16:30; Psalms 93:1; 96:10; 104:5), therefore the sun revolved around the earth. Galileo refuted this doctrine of Christian teaching and stated that not only does the earth move, but also, the sun is at the center of the universe, and thus the earth revolves around the sun. The whole of this problem within the church is that scientific research creates contention between religion and science that persists in various forms today.

As I embark upon this research I will address the issue of social justice within the Black church and how I perceive that the Black church of the twenty-first century continues to veer left of what we historically have considered justice issues. I will look at the contemporary and historical framework of the church and examine how women have fit into, or been excluded from, that framework. This examination will focus on the lives of prominent female preachers but also include the broader scope of women's service in the church past and present. Finally, I will offer some insight to current ministry perspectives through interviews conducted with female ministers in various capacities in the community in which I serve.

My research focus is a nexus between the place that I loved and a place that loved me—the Black church and social justice. The history of the Negro church in America has an intrinsically deep and valuable history that spans across three centuries with varying nuances of African tribal religion within the fabric of the experience.

When speaking of the Black church I speak of the oneness of the Black church universally, which should not be confused with making the Black church a monolithic institution; for we are as diverse as the very nature of Christianity and humanity.

Religious history is an important aspect in the formation of this research. In Africa, the use of the Sankofa bird symbolizes looking back toward history to get a better understanding of who one is, as an important aspect of African American culture and religious practices.[1] The "Black church" ontologically and spiritually is a different institution than the "White church."

As with the identity of the Africans in slavery, the Black church is as diverse and as steeped in culture as the continent from which the slaves were stolen. When speaking of the "Black church" we are talking about the "sociological and theological shorthand reference to the pluralism of black Christian churches in the United States."[2] The "Black church" has grown exponentially since the African slave's freedom. Congregations have gathered themselves into denominations and conventions. The oldest church is the African Methodist Episcopal Church (AME), organized in 1787 as the Free African Society in Philadelphia, Pennsylvania, by Richard Allen[3]—the largest being the National Baptist Convention, USA, which was founded in 1880 in Montgomery, Alabama, with more than seven million adherents in 2010.[4]

---
1. Akan language of Ghana meaning "reach back to look forward."
2. C. Eric Lincoln and Lawrence H. Mamiya, *The Black Church in the African American Experience* (Durham, NC: Duke University Press, 1990), 1.
3. Ibid., 1.
4. http://www.thearda.com/rcms2010/Blackprot.asp. Accessed December 1, 2016.

It was in church where Black men and women in America were able to find a spiritual (and sometimes physical) home when this country declared we were less than human. In an interview about the Black church, comedian Dick Gregory says, "The bulletin at the Black church was my *New York Times*; it was my *Time* magazine." The church bulletin as he puts it "told the news of the community that I lived in . . ." He goes on to say,

> . . . the Black church was my daddy, the Black church was where I went to school, the Black church was my camp, it was my . . . Santa Claus. . . . I sit and listen to these new stats today that 85% of all children that drown in America today is African American and 90% of their mothers and father can't swim. Why? Because when I grew up you couldn't go to the white YMCA where they had a swimming pool; you couldn't go to the city swimming pool. When they make a whole race of people invisible, I'll wear green, blue, chartreuse; in order for you to laugh at me you have to see me! So I came here to the [Black] church and became visible![5]

The Black church, the backbone of our community, is a sacred institution for Africans living in America. The Black church has been a place of transformation yet also a place of tragedy; a place of liberation yet a place of limitation; a place of healing yet a place of hurt.

The Black church is the oldest institution owned by Black people in this nation, yet the Black church has very few people writing its history. In this nation, for more than two hundred years, it was illegal for a Black person to read, let alone write, so the history of our people and the history of our churches had to be carried down through oral tradition.

My worldview and epistemology has been strongly influenced by the narratives and traditions of the church in which I was reared and nurtured. My worldview has been informed by my collective church experiences. I have had many life challenges that continue to expand my view on ministry. Having been preaching for more than four decades, my understanding of ministry has evolved, grown, and changed.

When I first started preaching I was a teenager going about ministry through my understanding and worldview as a Baptist. I was not privy to a diverse understanding of ministry but was pigeonholed into a way of

---

5. https://www.youtube.com/watch?v=0-2n5uNsunU. Accessed July 23, 2025.

thinking then, that eventually, over time, I learned was not totally in sync with my growing understanding of ministry.

Time and tradition tell us that in the beginning of Black Christian preaching in America, Black men preached to more White audiences than they did to Black audiences.[6] This is for several reasons. First, some Whites did not believe that Blacks were human, therefore Blacks were unable to be saved. If they could not be saved then there was no need to preach to them. Second, if Whites did believe that Blacks were human and could be saved, then what the Black people heard from the Bible had to be censored and limited in order to keep the institution of slavery intact.

Allowing slaves to preach imbued them with a certain level of "responsibility," which would therefore earn greater respect from other slaves. In this, the Black preacher had both position and power. Not only had he been sent by God, but he also had been entrusted by his White master to preach to the Black slaves. This dynamic of respect and regard is still active in some Black Baptist churches today. In his book *God's Trombones,* James Weldon Johnson said this about the Black preacher:

> *The old-time preacher was generally a man far above the average in intelligence; he was, not infrequently, a man of positive genius. The earliest of these preachers must have virtually committed many parts of the Bible to memory through hearing the scriptures read or preached from in the white churches which the slaves attended. They were the first of the slaves to learn to read, and their reading was confined to the Bible, and specifically to the more dramatic passages of the Old Testament. A text served mainly as a starting point and often had no relation to the development of the sermon. Nor would the old-time preacher balk at any text within the lids of the Bible.*[7]

Although the Black preacher and the Black church in the twenty-first century is no longer under the oppressive, watchful eye of a master, many congregants still revere and regard their pastors with a similar sense of awe and respect. The pastor is seen in a light of honor and respect because of the title and the position he holds.

---

6. John W. Blassingame, *The Slave Community: Plantation Life in the Antebellum South* (New York: Oxford University Press, 1979), 132.
7. James Weldon Johnson, *God's Trombones: Seven Negro Sermons in Verse* (New York: Penguin Classics, 1976), 4.

Dwight Hopkins' scholarship brings to light the dynamics within the slave-master relationship, regarding spiritual direction of the slave and the importance of keeping the slave preacher under the control of the master by the slave master's actions and words.[8]

The understanding of the call to preach, in both the twenty-first and nineteenth centuries, is important for this work as well. The "call" for Black and White preachers in America has historically been different.[9] Being called in the Black Baptist tradition historically has meant that one encountered God, and God expressly told that person to go about doing something for the kingdom of God on the earth. This is where the calls of both Blacks and Whites seem to coincide.

However, in the Black Baptist tradition, not only does God call the preacher, but also, the community must confirm this call after witnessing the actions and the testimony of the preacher. In the Black Baptist church, historically, this is a "both-and" method. If God has truly called you, as people in the Black Baptist tradition believe, then your call should "show some signs" and be accepted by the very people God has sent you to lead.

Black preaching, especially amongst slaves, was a different kind of preaching. This preaching would later be called radical and take on the moniker "prophetic preaching." Homiletician and Black preacher Cleophus LaRue said, "To get at the heart of black preaching, one has to understand the interconnectedness between scriptural texts and African American life experiences."[10]

While White men were preaching doctrine, dogma, and pious living to their congregations and to their slaves, the slave preacher was forced to preach with a different spiritual dispensation, that spoke truth to power and often went against the very laws of the land in which they lived.[11] While White slave owners spent a great amount of time preaching to keep slaves subordinate and obedient to the laws of the land, slaves understood the Bible and Christianity differently; the Bible's verses were meant to liberate, not oppress them.[12]

---

8. Dwight N. Hopkins, *Down, Up, and Over: Slave Religion and Black Theology* (Minneapolis, Minnesota: Fortress Press, 2000), 51.
9. Love Henry Whelchel, *Hell Without Fire: Conversion in Slave Religion* (Nashville, TN: Abingdon Press, 2002), 78-79.
10. Cleophus LaRue, *The Heart of Black Preaching* (Louisville, KY: Westminster John Knox Press, 1999), 13.
11. Henry H. Mitchell, *Black Preaching* (New York: Harper & Row, 1979), 68.
12. Blassingame, *The Slave Community*, 132.

When explaining Black preaching from a scholarly perspective in the *Scholar of Black Preaching*, Rev. Henry H. Mitchell says that Black preaching has its own hermeneutic.[13] This hermeneutic is the foundation of the theology that the Black preacher and the Black church inhabits, and from this comes Black Liberation Theology. Mitchell says the following:

> *The Black ancestors felt no compulsion to be orthodox or accepted. They showed no inclination to follow literalistic interpretations such as those devised to justify slavery. On the contrary, they looked without vested bias for answers to Black people's needs. They took the Bible extremely seriously, but they never condoned slavery. Their spirituals attest to the fact that they seized on the Moses narrative and sang, "Tell ol' Pharaoh to let my people go!" When they sang about "stealing away," they no doubt had some notion of the prayer closet, but there is strong reason to believe that to steal away to Jesus was also to escape to freedom! Similarly, to sing "I ain't got long to stay here" is not exclusively other-worldly escape. It is the code language of the gospel of self-liberation.*[14]

Even in the context of this liberation theology—the crux of Black theology since the 1960s—women have remained a largely oppressed population in the Black church. Women, while constituting the majority of the membership in Black churches across all denominations, have been denied access to power and ministry leadership.[15] It is a strange paradox that women have been barred from the pulpit but are depended upon by churches "for the bulk of their regular attendance, financial support, and general church work."[16]

This intersection of gender, church leadership, and spirituality has been the birthing ground for much debate in the church at-large. In one account, Works Progress Administration worker Alvin N. Canon walked into a Pentecostal church in Chicago where "Mrs. Williams" had assumed leadership over a congregation after the death of her husband. When he asked Mrs. Williams about what distinguished her independent Pentecostal church from others, she provided a remarkable answer:

---

13. Henry H. Mitchell, *Black Preaching: The Recovery of a Powerful Art* (Nashville, TN: Abingdon Press, 1990), 20.
14. Ibid., 20-21.
15. Wallace Best, "The Spirit of the Holy Ghost is a Male Spirit: African American Preaching Women and the Paradoxes of Gender," in *Women and Religion in the African Diaspora. Knowledge, Power and Performance*, R. Marie Griffith and Barbara Dianne Savage, eds. (Baltimore: Hopkins University Press, 2006), 101.
16. Ibid., 101.

> *Well, the Church of God in Christ says that only men can preach—women can only do missionary work. Well, in a sense they are right because according to the Bible the spirit of the Holy Ghost is a male spirit. But when a woman receives that spirit she is no longer a woman—then she has the right to perform the duties of a man, like preaching. Until then she should only do missionary work and teaching work. The word of God is a "he" and women are the flesh of the world. . . . Now I believe that some people are both with a unity to God. These people are devoted to the work of the Lord—they don't have time to think about sex and the things of the world.*[17]

While there is much that can be unpacked from this response, it is particularly rife with much of the struggle that women would face in the church historically, and even into contemporary church life. First, as the Word of God does, it makes a differentiation between the flesh and the spirit. However, by Mrs. Williams' definition, women are the "flesh of the world." The Bible draws clear lines between the flesh and the spirit, and the inability of the two to function in tandem.

The flesh is condemned as being against the spirit and a hindrance to spiritual and religious progression. As Romans 8:8 states, *"Those who are in the flesh cannot please God."*[18] Under this definition, women are inherently at a spiritual disadvantage toward progress because of the nature of their bodies.

This theme has carried throughout history and into the contemporary culture of the Black church where men, even in sexually immoral or compromised positions, are easily forgiven while women are vilified, ostracized, and demoralized for the same actions.[19] Men's bodies do not stand in the way of their spirituality or their ability to practice religion and preach, whereas women's bodies are a hindrance and a stumbling block under this definition—classifying them as more prone to sin.[20] Black women in particular were critically scrutinized under this mindset due to the nature of race relations in America.

Up until the second century, women were leaders of the early church. However, by the fourth century, church order reflected the rejection of

---
17. Ibid., 104.
18. Romans 8:8 (NRSVUE)
19. Best, 107.
20. Ibid., 106.

female leadership by patriarchal society.[21] The *Didascalia Apostolorum* stated that since women were not explicitly appointed by Jesus to teach and prophesy, then they were disqualified from those services. Of course, women were identified with the apostles and could therefore be a part of ministry, but they were not allowed to teach or lead in any capacity.[22] The issue here was not explicitly with women in ministry, but with women in leadership, which many supposed went against the original order from Jesus Christ and the early Pauline teachings.[23]

So, after the original growth boom of the church, women became relegated to specific positions and categorically banned from leadership in many ways. In response to this, some women flocked to convents and other ascetic lifestyles where they could be free from the demands of domesticity and live a life fully devoted to spiritual pursuits while also able to secure leadership in these convents and orders.[24] For contemporary women in leadership, particularly Black women, they have to contend with issues of gender, race, and classism that all intersect on the pulpit.[25]

These issues were exasperated through the conditions in America where gender, race, and class collided constantly. While a rise in domesticity correlating with greater capitalism in America allowed the White woman to blossom as a symbol of virtue, home, and family, Black women were not afforded this same classification. In fact, by the late 1800s, the stereotype of the "lascivious, promiscuous, and morally corrupt Black woman had congealed in the white mind."[26] This was exacerbated by the historical stigma associated with Black women's bodies due to the long history of White men claiming unmitigated access to them.[27] Black women in the public sphere, particularly in the church, had to continuously reclaim their femininity and brand it as virtuous.

There are a number of accounts, including those of Sojourner Truth, Jarena Lee, and Maria Stewart (prominent Black female preachers), that had to contend with outward pressure questioning their very womanhood and inward pressure from their denominations that often questioned their spirituality.

---

21. Vashti M. McKenzie, *Not Without a Struggle: Leadership Development for African American Women in Ministry—Revised and Updated* (Cleveland, Ohio: Pilgrim Press, 2012), 47.
22. Ibid., 49.
23. Ibid., 52.
24. Ibid., 51.
25. Ibid., 58.
26. Best, 107.
27. Ibid., 108.

Furthermore, the Black female preacher has often been critiqued for her sexuality, while Black male ministers have not. Not just historically, but even in contemporary society, waywardness, sexual immorality, and depravity have been witnessed and forgiven, and have seen the offender restored when the offender is a Black male preacher. Not so with Black female preachers. The issue of gender and body politics is one that has followed Black female preachers since they began preaching and continues in contemporary debate. For some women, this struggle with sexuality has compelled them to navigate their gender in interesting ways.

The first option to navigate gender is to reject it altogether and assume "mannish" demeanor. Those who have taken this route attempt to mimic male leadership by taking on male mannerisms, dressing austerely, and avoiding all references or insinuations that they are gendered at all. In some cases, this has led to speculation about the sexuality and nature of relationships between women leaders and other women under their ministry.

Such were rumors that developed about Mary Evans, a prominent Chicago minister who began her ministry in Chicago in 1932. Evans never spoke about her sexuality and she never married. Despite this, she maintained two long-term relationships with women that included aspects of working together and even joint living arrangements. Although the census lists them as sisters, it was clear to parishioners and others in the community that they were not related. Some biographers speculate that this designation could refer to them commonly as "sisters in Christ" as many church women were wont to do at that time.[28] Despite the curiosities about Evans' lifestyle and what community members described as her "mannish" ways, she was a very influential church and community activist in the Chicago community during the height of her service. Although she did not drive for racial equality and race issues from the pulpit, her church held the most drives and recruited the largest number of new members to the NAACP.

Black women have laid claim to the call to preach for many years. A number of prominent historical female preachers have emerged. One such preacher is Jarena Lee. In the anthology *Sisters of the Spirit*, Jarena Lee, Zilpha Elaw, and Julia Foote lay out their autobiographies. These three women, though distinct in their experiences, share common threads of religious experience.

---

28. Ibid., 114.

Jarena Lee, whose life will be further elaborated in chapter 2 of this discourse, was an African Methodist Episcopal (A.M.E.) preacher whose conversion experience compelled her to find joy in the Creator of her soul. She was able to find expression of that joy in serving in the A.M.E. church in Philadelphia, where she was able to live out her call to "the Christ that smiles."[29]

All three women, similarly, experienced redemption and conversion experiences where they went through a period of realizing the depth of their own sin, struggling for redemption, being granted redemption, and rejoicing in their justification.[30]

Black women's stories of and participation in the church have added color and tone to Black theology and its counterparts such as liberation theology.

One way in which women have reclaimed their stories in the midst of the liberation gospel narrative from which they have, as a class, been excluded is to find their voice in the midst of biblical text. Eboni Turman relates what she felt when she first encountered the repositioning of the story of Hagar as a narrative to which Black and oppressed women could relate:

> *My discovery of the second tradition of African American biblical appropriation excited me greatly. This tradition emphasized female activity and de-emphasized male authority. It lifted up from the Bible the story of a female slave of African descent.... For more than 100 years Hagar—the African slave of the Hebrew woman Sarah—has appeared in the deposits of African American culture. Sculptors, writers, poets, scholars, preachers and just plain folks have passed along the biblical figure Hagar to generation after generation of Black folks....*[31]

Just as the crux of much of Black liberation theology has hinged on the story of the Israelites' journey from slavery in Egypt to freedom found

---

29. Karen Baker-Fletcher, *Sisters Struggling in the Spirit: A Women of Color Theological Anthology* (Louisville, Kentucky: Women's Ministries Program Area, National Ministries Division, and Christian Faith and Life Program Area, Congregational Ministries Division, Presbyterian Church (U.S.A.), 1994), 34.
30. Ibid., 36.
31. Eboni Turman, *Toward a Womanist Ethic of Incarnation: Black Bodies, the Black Church, and the Council of Chalcedon* (New York: Palgrave Macmillan, 2013), 141.

in the Promised Land after a journey through the wilderness, Black women can find voice in the story of Hagar and her pleas to God to save her child when they were exiled to the wilderness at her mistress's request. For many Black women, they may find themselves in the mirror of Hagar's story as it may be truer to their experience in that "the oppressed and abused do not always experience God's liberating power."[32] For many Black women who echo mantras of "making a way out of no way" and "doing the best you can," Hagar's story may be a more realistic view of life than that of making it to the Promised Land.

Unfortunately, also for many women, both inside and outside of the church, their life is characterized by their ability to consistently make a dollar out of fifteen cents. They face struggles from the professional arena to their home life and find little to no rest for their weary souls.

In fact, womanist theologian Dolores Williams asserts that the Black woman's role in the history of the United States has much in common with the narrative of Hagar. Hagar was a woman who was from an oppressed class whose body was used to perform the purpose of her oppressors. In this case, she was forced to be the surrogate to her master Abraham at the behest of his wife, Sarah. Particularly in slave narrative and interaction with the White over-class, Black women are and have been types of Hagars throughout history, going so far as to suffer rape at the hands of their White owners and having to nurse and care for the children of the White families that laid claim to their bodies and their personhood.

Hagar's personhood can further be seen as subjugated by "the divine authority that intervenes not on her behalf but on the behalf of the interests of the Black male child. The validity of this perspective is amplified in Hagar's second wilderness experience when God attends to Hagar's distress only because of God's primary 'hearing' of Ishmael's cry."[33]

We do not see rescue and prosperity in Hagar's story; nonetheless we see a type of redemption. Turman writes, "Hagar was not engaged by a God who liberated her from the deplorable social circumstances to which she was captive, but rather by a God who provided resources for her to negotiate a quality of life that empowered her to survive the brokenness of her social circumstances."[34]

---

32. Ibid., 142.
33. Ibid., 143.
34. Ibid., 142.

Black Woman as Mother in the Community

For many Black women, their early roles in the church mimicked their roles within the family and the community. When Africans were brought to America, it was not only their bodies that were affected by the Middle Passage. They lost their culture, social structures, familial ties, and their homeland.[35] However, the ethic of family-hood survived and the term "Mother" was imbued with a sense of respect, leadership, and community responsibility.

In the secular realm, a Mother could be a prominent community figure, head of a Black woman's organization, and/or someone who wielded clout with a number of community organizations. In the religious sphere, Mothers were often pastors' wives, widows, group leaders, and sometimes even the pastors themselves.[36] In these spheres, Black women were not tangential, they were not merely supportive figures, but they led, administered, and ran these organizations. While early church development may have barred them from the ministry, they nevertheless were able to garner significant power through lay participation and respect within the community.[37] In fact,

> *The roles of church and community mothers represent impositions of familistic and pseudo-familistic ties upon social organizations and the process of social influence. These mothers serve effectively for a very long time and accumulate great prestige and, in many cases, very real authority. Not only are they role models, power brokers, and venerable elders, but the actuarial realities of Black life are such that elderly Black women provide the continuity necessary to promote unity in the face of ever-changing historical conditions* . . . .[38]

Remarkable to note and born of necessity, in an era when the lives of many Black men were threatened, extinguished, and male leaders ran the risk of attracting attention and being jailed, killed, or lynched, the role of the Black Mother in the community (as one who holds everything together) was absolutely essential. She would maintain continuity and progression even as the turnover of visible community leaders and participants was frequent. The role of the Mother in community was very much tied to her role in the church and extended her realm of influence from the streets to the pulpit and beyond.

---

35. Cheryl T. Gilkes, *If It Wasn't for the Women . . .: Black Women's Experience and Womanist Culture in Church and Community* (New York: Orbis Books, 2000), 61.
36. Ibid.
37. Ibid., 62.
38. Ibid., 63.

One sphere in which Black women were allowed to serve influential and important leadership roles in the church was Sunday school. Sunday school was born out of concern for impoverished children. Due to working long hours for their families, children were often illiterate and uneducated. They lacked basic skills of reading and writing. Not only did this lack of education not assist them in their current state, but it also ensured that any progress they could possibly make would be limited by their lack of skills and knowledge.

In the beginning, the Sunday school movement was opposed. Sunday was reserved for church and that was it. Despite male leadership's admission that there was an issue, they were reluctant to allow Sunday school. Nevertheless, due to the tireless work of women, Sunday school was implemented and began to flourish. It should be noted that the historic Sunday school is not as we think of it today, as an extension of the church service with attention to biblical study, much like a Bible study. Sunday school was, in fact, a traditional school that was administered on Sunday.

Sunday school taught work skills, reading, writing, and arithmetic to those who were unfortunate enough to be unable to take part in traditional education. This effort was largely driven and supplied by the women who organized the schools and supplied the teachers. In fact, the success of this schooling, and the fact that it was largely supplied and driven by women, is the reason that some opposition persisted.[39]

The Sunday school movement was successful. As it gained more acceptance and power, as had been seen at times in the past (such as with the Missionary movement), male leadership took over and put a formal hand of organization over it. Eventually men fully assumed leadership of the organization and it became a formal structure of the church.

The Church Mother of old was revered, respected, and protected. She was a source of spiritual wisdom, not just to the congregation, but to the pastor as well. She was trusted and may or may not have had titular leadership but was looked to as a moral compass and sage of the congregation.[40]

The Mother figure still persists in contemporary Black churches where older women and widows are considered Mothers in the church. In many instances, they oversee the sacred ordinances such as holy Communion,

---

39. Stanley Grenz and Denise Kjesbo, *Women in the Church: A Biblical Theology of Women in Ministry* (Lisle, Illinois: InterVarsity Press, 1995), 45.
40. Gilkes, 103.

baptism, christening, and the means of salvation. These Mothers are often on church boards and/or committees, such as hospitality, church care, and deacon/deaconess board. Without these positions the church would be lacking order and decorum for some of their most sacred rituals.

The Mothers of the church were also in charge of teaching the younger women how to assume these positions and fill the roles.

Black Women as Leaders of the Church

Despite much of the oppression of Black women in the church, Black women have risen as church leaders. Contemporary patriarchal models would emphasize the stories of wayward or irredeemable women in the Bible, the favorite of these being Jezebel. Both the Old and the New Testaments are full of examples of women in leadership (i.e., Deborah [see Judges 4], Naomi and Ruth [see Ruth 1], Shiphrah and Puah [see Exodus 1], Miriam [see Exodus], Huldah [see 2 Kings 22], Phoebe [see Romans 16], Anna [see Luke 2], daughters of Philip [see Acts 21], the woman at the well [see John 4], Lydia [see Acts 16], and a host of others)—both named and unnamed in the biblical text.

While the letters of Paul have been used to silence women in the congregation, his letters are also permeated with examples and praise of women doing ministry (in many forms), across many (if not all) of the congregations under his care. Women in leadership is not new to God, but it seems to be a difficult pill for many men in leadership to swallow.

Vashti McKenzie offers a great conceptualization of women's leadership in her work *Not Without a Struggle*.[41] She posits that leadership must be redesigned to fit the model of women in ministry, particularly of Black women in ministry. Women bring unique characteristics to leadership, such as nurturing others, encouraging participation, sharing power and information, creating positive work spaces, and empowering others.[42]

While male leadership models have been the predominant paradigm for governance, many times these models are not native, organic, or advantageous for women. Instead, women can begin from their own experience and develop leadership models that work for them and in their context. McKenzie offers a number of models for contemporary women in ministerial leadership.

---
41. McKenzie, 68.
42. Ibid., 70.

Sister Girlfriend is a woman who is an active member of many groups and thrives on community and friendship. She is a woman who enjoys working with others and prefers it as her mode of operation. Her life, her home, and her office are always filled with people. She may not be very productive and places a deep value on personal relationships over tasks.[43]

The Queen does not just take charge but she rules over any domain she is given. Her desire is to see obedience in her congregation, in the affiliate leadership, and in the organization. She is very task-oriented and everyone knows who is boss.[44]

Mama embodies the leader that keeps everyone organized—from the youngest member to the oldest participant. This leadership style ranks high in relationships and tasks. The Mama is excellent at making sure that everyone is doing their job and doing it well. True to her name, she nurtures the congregation into spiritual maturity by entrusting them with tasks and allowing them to do them.

Wise Woman (referred to as the Zoe in some African traditions), is the wisdom keeper. Often people look up to her for her knowledge and understanding. The Wise Woman seems to effortlessly navigate murky waters without being tainted. She may be more of a loner and keep to herself, but she is sought as a resource. She is both a low relationship and low task-oriented kind of leader.[45]

Sapphire is determined and fueled by a sense of duty and responsibility. She stands out in any crowd, much like a sapphire stone. Sapphires are driven to perfection, the first time, and therefore may be workaholics. She is goal-oriented, in charge, and driven.[46]

Finessa is able to be commanding like Sapphire but does so with much more tact. She is able to organize, work hard, and perfect how the organization is run. She can be described as sassy, smooth, and embodying excellent people skills. She can best be described as the "iron fist in the velvet glove."[47]

McKenzie also describes the *Liberationist*, who believes and espouses liberation theology, the *Africentrist* who can easily be identified by her

---

43. Ibid., 95.
44. Ibid., 96.
45. Ibid., 97.
46. Ibid., 98.
47. Ibid., 100.

afro-centered garb and rhetoric, the *Chameleon* who is adept at adapting to any situation as needed, and the *Yo, Baby, Yo* leader who has a tough background and is able to get down and dirty when necessary to maintain her leadership position.[48]

Women in current ministry leadership embody one (or more) of these styles of leadership. Each classification embraces the unique qualities of women to some degree. Most women, reading these descriptions, will recognize themselves in one or several of these categories, in some form. These female-driven leadership roles embrace the feminine and emphasize those traits that make women particularly suited to leadership in ministry.

That a scholar could even venture to write about women from such diverse perspectives is a departure from the past in and of itself. Previously, women were not thought of as having value or recognized for their diverse gifts. Now that women are breaking into academic fields and birthing their own movement, they are able to tell their stories and have them honored in true womanist fashion.

Despite the many obstacles in the way of Black women assuming leadership in the church, there nonetheless remains undeniable evidence that they are an integral and important part of church life. Whether historically or contemporarily, women have worked at the heart of the Black church to provide support, help, order, beauty, and structure. All of their efforts have contributed to progress in whatever facet they may have functioned. From "the implementation of Women's Day . . . the Black women's club movement, and the women's boards that emerge from the dual-sex politics of the Black church as principal illustrations of how Black church women have continued to flourish in spite of the overwhelming sexism they continue to confront." In fact, Cheryl Townsend Gilkes goes so far as to say, "If it wasn't for the women, Black men wouldn't have a church."[49]

In this assertion, she places Black women not just IN the church but at the very center and heart of church life. Despite their considerable struggles with leadership, sexism, and discrimination, it nonetheless remains that they have established themselves as a force within the church. Imagine if no obstacle had been placed in their way what more could have been achieved for the kingdom!

---

48. Ibid., 101.
49. Gilkes, 1.

Black women in leadership roles in the church have also had to wade through considerable oppression regarding which positions of leadership they were capable of assuming. For instance, it was all right for a woman to be the head of the usher board or the hospitality committee or the Sunday school, but assuming rank in any level of clerical leadership was thought to be out of the question. Nonetheless, despite much of the considerable opposition that women have faced in traditional ministry and particularly in leadership, a number of historical women paved the way for prominent contemporary women preachers and ministry leaders today.

Chapter 2

Black Women: Willing Workers

Much of the question of identity and background of women in the church has been explicated in chapter 1. There were and continue to be a number of factors surrounding gender, social roles, and interpretation of biblical theology that have at times empowered, and at times oppressed, women in church and particularly women in church leadership roles. Even though these issues can be broadly defined, they vary a bit from denomination to denomination. It may be helpful to look at two of the traditional major denominations (Baptist and Methodist) and the evolution of women in their ranks.

Baptist

In early Baptist tradition, the power and aptitude of women in missions was wholly recognized. As early as 1871, Baptist women had begun to organize The Women's Baptist Foreign Missionary Society of the West, which was geared toward mission work in Africa. The headquarters of this organization was in Chicago. Louise C. Fleming became the first woman missionary to travel extensively overseas in Africa and the Congo.[50]

This effort soon trickled into other areas of the Baptist church and organizations began to spring up. Under the leadership of Rev. W. J. Simmons, The Baptist Women's Educational Convention of the State of Kentucky was organized with three objectives: encourage youth to attend state college under the direction of Rev. Simmons, contribute money to paying off debt on the State College property, and encourage mission work on behalf of their organization.[51]

Seeing the success of this organization and the ways in which they worked to support other institutions, religious leaders soon adopted the model and began educational and missionary societies in other locations (i.e., Alabama, Arkansas, and Georgia).[52] A number of women moved in the direction of foreign missions from these local missionary societies.

---
50. Leroy Fitts, *A History of Black Baptists* (Nashville, TN: Broadman Press, 1985), 121.
51. Ibid, 122.
52. Ibid, 123.

Women (such as Mamie Branton, Nora Gordon, E. B. Delaney, etc.) spread faith and Baptist denominationalism across Africa. They traveled to regions such as Liberia, South Africa, Congo, and other areas of Central and Western Africa.[53]

In 1912 (endorsed by the Foreign Mission Board of the National Baptist Convention, USA, Inc.), Susie Taylor founded the Baptist Industrial Academy in Liberia, which was the second-largest school under the jurisdiction of the Convention. This was considerable work because land had to be selected, purchased, and developed, buildings constructed, and all aspects of the school had to be administrated.[54]

This school represented just the beginning of the legacy of women in mission work in the Baptist Convention. Hospitals would be built, relief programs would be organized, orphanages would be opened, schools and other educational facilities would be constructed, and a myriad of women, their spouses, and their families would provide aid to ailing African communities and meet the numerous needs they saw there. Historically, their efforts were so successful that missions have come to be known as a greatly influential field for women in the Baptist Convention.[55]

For women seeking roles outside of Baptist mission work, the road to recognition has been a bit harder. It wasn't until 1979 that the Baptist Ministers Conference of Baltimore, led by Rev. Vernon Dobson, admitted women to its membership. That year, three women ministers were admitted to fellowship: Rev. Lydia Starks, Rev. Minnie Robinson, and Rev. Agnes M. Alston.[56] This move did not transpire without opposition. The Washington, D.C., Conference severed ties with the Baltimore Conference.

With this new change, women began to submit their memberships and even local churches ordained more women for ministry.[57] Some churches, such as St. John's Baptist Church in Columbia, South Carolina, even began to ordain women as deacons, which was previously unheard of.[58] The perpetrator of this action, Rev. Eaton, had to defend himself as serving a God that does not judge usefulness based upon sexual gender, but that all are able to be servants equally.[59]

---

53. Ibid., 125.
54. Ibid., 126.
55. Ibid., 134.
56. Ibid., 310.
57. Ibid.
58. Ibid., 311.
59. Ibid., 313.

While women were being ordained and more accepted, they were still only equal in title at the very least. Very few women got called to preach (aside from special Women's Day services) or participate in tangential aspects of church life. Rarely, if ever, were they allowed to be a normalized centerpiece. As further movements of feminism, liberation, and ecumenism emerge, they will call out denominations to "catch up." Women continue to become increasingly involved in church leadership and in aspects of the liturgical and preaching moments.[60]

Methodist

Much of the Methodist movement for women was greatly influenced by outside political and social pressures of the times. By 1880, the "woman question" was at the forefront of many discussions of Methodist polity and practice. While there are a number of distinctions between the three largest groups of Methodism (African Methodist Episcopal, African Methodist Episcopal Zion, and the Colored Methodist Episcopal Church), each was wrestling with what it meant for women to serve, and in what capacities they should serve post-slavery.[61]

In post-Civil War and Reconstruction Era America, equality, unity, and emphasis of obtaining rights was on the forefront of the agenda for American Black leaders. The added pressure of including women promoted and pushed by women's groups pressed religious organizations to solidify unity on the issues of race, which often meant conceding, in some ways, for the rights of women.[62] This was an optimistic time of rebuilding.

While women formerly were given very little authority or titular recognition, though they comprised major percentages of many fundraising and church support organizations, post-war Methodism saw them preaching, teaching, voting, and holding offices in decision-making bodies within the church. In the 1870s, the *Disciplines* of both Black Methodist denominations were modified to give women the same rights as men within the body of the church.[63]

The founding of missionary societies put women in places of action and power. However, church bylaws still required the election of men to the boards of such societies. In these capacities, women were afforded

---
60. Ibid., 314.
61. Martha Jones, "Make Us a Power," in *Women and Religion in the African Diaspora: Knowledge, Power, and Performance* (Baltimore, Maryland: John Hopkins University Press, 2006), 129.
62. Ibid., 149.
63. Ibid., 135.

limited exercise of autonomy. Although no opposition was openly formed, they remained restricted and opposed when waters were tested.[64]

Behind the optimism of Reconstruction came an opposing social force exacted on the church with the dawning of the Jim Crow Era. Previous rights that were held by Blacks were stripped away, the forward movement of the Reconstruction was halted, and new ways were devised to oppress, cripple, and kill Black communities. These pressures directly affected the church.

In the General Conference of 1888, the A.M.E. church formally amended their *Discipline* to bar women from holding the office of bishop. Almost a decade later, the issue of women's ordination would arise in the A.M.E. Zion Church when Bishop Charles Pettey ordained Deacon Mary Small to the station of elder.[65] This would bring the woman question to the forefront and cause division and great argument within the body. In this debate, proponents on each side vocalized their opinions. Those in favor of women's ordination argued political equality of women and their capacity to do work in ministry based upon previous merits.[66] Those opposed to the ordination of women argued fear of changing the historically male-ordered hierarchy of the church, the inability and frailty of women to operate in all seasons and on all occasions, the inherent weakness of the female gender, and the "unsexing" of women by elevating them to the office of elder.[67]

As Black men on the political scene were losing power and becoming more marginalized, they scrambled for ways to regain a sense of authority. In the church, men vied for the little portion of public authority that remained to them, which existed in the hierarchal, male-dominated ranks of the church.[68] Martha Jones writes,

> *Although the A.M.E. Zion debate reflected long-standing permutations of the woman question, within and outside the church, one aspect of the ordination controversy was new, reflecting tensions among male church leaders that were generated by the collapse of the Reconstruction and the rise of the Jim Crow order of the 1890's. The debate became terrain*

---

64. Ibid., 138.
65. Ibid., 145.
66. Ibid., 147.
67. Ibid., 148.
68. Ibid., 149.

> upon which men on both sides of the question manifested their differences with one another. Through the deployment of metaphors of combat and violence, critiques of men's capacities as ministers, challenges to the church's hierarchical structure and shows of intellectual prowess, A.M.E. Zion's male leaders vied for what little public authority had been left to them. What began as the woman question during the optimistic climate of Reconstruction became, with the degradations of Jim Crow, the man question . . . the pervasive use of metaphors of combat and violence was the first hint that church men had more at stake in the debate than the standing of women. . . ."[69]

Indeed, Black men within these institutions fought tooth and nail, not simply against the elevation of women, but in response to their own social subjugation. By 1898, this debate had become so rancorous and divisive that leading bishops feared it would divide the church irreparably. In response to this, they united on the idea that women's rights within the church should reflect their political standing within society, thus they were entitled to autonomy and authority, to a degree.[70]

These tensions in the A.M.E. Church continued to persist. A.M.E. Zion churches elected their first female bishops in 2002 and 2008, respectively. Even with this overdue expansion in the role of women in Methodist ministry, much work remains to be done in equality between the sexes within the four walls of the church.

There are various times in society that marked and influenced the direction of the church as well. Industrialization had a major influence on all denominations, not just Black denominations—but the effects are felt there as well. In pre-industrial society, the warrior/hunter theme characterized "manly" roles where aggression and competitiveness were considered central traits of masculinity. Once the industrial revolution was in full swing, many jobs that men did no longer embodied these characteristics. Instead, men were in factories or linemen doing relatively safe jobs that did not require much brute strength. As a result, the masculine persona of the "breadwinner" was born. Now, it was considered masculine to be a provider for the family, regardless of how one came about those provisions; and, therefore, women's roles were restricted to the home

---

69. Ibid.
70. Ibid., 152.

where they could not interfere with the "breadwinning" the men needed to do.[71] So, work became a "battleground" and home became a refuge. Women became religious agents and a "feminization of the church accompanied the divinization of the home."[72] Male clergy found it increasingly difficult to reach their male audience with the de-masculinization of religion and therefore began an orchestrated suppression of women in the church sphere. In order to reclaim masculinity and reassert the power of the church and clergy, women were again suppressed from leadership and ministerial roles.[73] This tendency was further exacerbated in the Black church because of the additional oppression that Black men experienced in society in general. Their claim to the religious sphere was their realm of unconstrained masculine influence.

The problem of this instinct to exhibit masculinity is pervasive and far-reaching. If being considered masculine is presupposed to be a requirement for leadership, then women are automatically excluded from the narrative based on sex alone. Eboni Turman discusses this:

> *Interestingly enough, behind the veil of race the moral problem of "making men," specifically toward the end of religious leadership exposes the problem of body not only as an intercommunal phenomenon emerging at the racialized edge of the color line, but as an intercommunal dilemma for Black people as well. Indeed, while "making men" presumes the circumscription of Black woman's identity to a primary nothingness because of her Blackness and class designation (similar to that of Black men) as proscribed by white supremacy, "making men" further stipulates that Black women cannot be "made" expressly because of their gendered identity. In other words, the intersection of race, gender, and class that Black women embody not only makes space for intercommunal theological, scientific, and social demonization of Black women to occur on the one hand, but more appallingly it allows room for intercommunal dehumanization to emerge, additionally subordinating Black women to Black men, on the other.*[74]

---

71. Grenz, 48.
72. Grenz, 48.
73. Grenz, 49.
74. Turman, 134.

Observing the historical influence and import of women throughout the Black church in the grand scheme has merit; however, it is also interesting to note that Black women have their own stories to tell as well. Jarena Lee, and her contemporary Zilpha Elaw, were two women of the Methodist tradition whose autobiographies and writings shed light on how women navigated not only the religious realm, but also the spiritual realm. These two early ministers paved the way for many women who came after them, both within their own denominations and in the church more broadly. They fought the fight to show that they were worthy, and that God, indeed, could call whomever He wanted to preach His Gospel, not only in spite of but also because they were women. Through taking a look at the lives of Jarena Lee, Zilpha Elaw, Prathia Hall, and Barbara Harris, we can see a picture of how women navigated their work in religious spheres and how the work evolved based upon era and opportunity.

Jarena Lee and Zilpha Elaw

Jarena Lee was born to a poor but free family on February 11, 1783, in New Jersey.[75] While much of Lee's autobiography, *Religious Experience and Journal of Mrs. Jarena Lee*, does not focus on her early life, she does admit that her parents had no knowledge of God and therefore did not teach her anything about Christianity.[76] When she was seven years old, she left home for a life of indentured servitude. It was during her time with the Sharp family as a servant that Jarena recalled recognizing the first move of the Holy Spirit within her. When asked by her mistress if she had completed some portion of work, she responded, "Yes," although she actually had not done it. Lee describes feeling the power of God move through her conscience and telling her what a wretched sinner she was. This movement of her conscience caused so much guilt that she was inspired to promise that she would never tell another lie.[77]

Although Lee accounts that God continued to strive with her, it wasn't until she reached age 21, in 1804, that she experienced another strong move of God. She was in attendance at a Presbyterian missionary service and was drawn by the reading of Psalms to realize her fallen nature and seek respite from it.

---
75. Blackpast.org, http://www.Blackpast.org/aah/lee-jarena-1783.
76. William Andrews (ed.), *Sisters of the Spirit: Three Black Women's Autobiographies of the Nineteeth Century* (Bloomington, IN: Indiana University Press, 1986), 27.
77. Ibid., 27.

Her search for spiritual peace eventually brought her to a Methodist church in Philadelphia, where Rev. Richard Allen was the pastor. During one of these services, after the preaching moment, Lee was so moved by the Spirit that she leapt from her seat and declared the forgiveness of God and the pardoning of sins. This moment is the moment that pins her full conversion.[78] Lee's experience in the Methodist church solidified her attendance and allegiance to the Methodist religious order.

For the next four years, Lee went through what can be called "a dark night of the soul." Many times she was plagued by thoughts of listlessness, powerlessness, and the weight of never being free from sin, wrestling with her flesh and thoughts that seemed to condemn her at every turn. More than once, she was on the precipice of taking her own life, and at the last moment she would be drawn away from the final act. Lee's spiritual condition soon manifested into a physical condition and she became ill. She was sent away to stay with a doctor, who was also a man of Methodist faith. It was during her time with him that she was able to come to an understanding of the Scriptures and find final rest in her salvation and the condition of her soul.[79]

In 1807, Lee acknowledged her call to preach and went to Bishop Richard Allen to make this confession. Unfortunately, he informed her that he could not grant her permission to preach, as he was required, by his station under the constitution of the Methodist Church, to forbid women to do so.[80] He, instead, encouraged her (as he admitted to doing for other women who professed the same) to engage in missionary work, exhortation, and leading of prayer meetings. Against such there was no law in the Methodist church.[81]

While Lee still felt the compulsion to preach the Gospel, her rejection by Allen served to deepen her faith. It caused her to seek God more fervently and with much more spiritual vigor. In the end, this setback only contributed to the deepening of her faith and affirmed her resolve that she was called to be a preacher.[82]

---

78. Ibid., 29.
79. Ibid., 31.
80. *Blackpast.org*.
81. Andrews, 36.
82. Ibid., 38.

In her autobiography, after the reflection of years, Lee expounds,

> *O how careful ought we to be, lest through our by-laws of church government and discipline, we bring into disrepute even the word of life. For as unseemly as it may appear now-a-days for a woman to preach, it should be remembered that nothing is impossible with God. Any why should it be thought impossible, heterodox, or improper, for a woman to preach? seeing the Saviour died for the woman as well as the man. If a man may preach, because the Saviour died for him, why not the woman? seeing he died for her also. Is he not a whole Saviour, instead of a half one?as those who hold it wrong for a woman to preach, would seem make it appear. Did not Mary first preach the risen Saviour, and is not the doctrine of the resurrection the very climax of Christianity—hangs not all our hope on this, as argued by St. Paul? Then did not Mary, a woman, preach the gospel? for she preached the resurrection of the crucified Son of God.*[83]

It is often in these ways that women had to find themselves in the Gospel and advocate for their involvement, plain though it should have been. This narrative is one that is repeated far too often when women have to defend their right to preach, teach, or sometimes even learn about the Gospel. Time and again we witness women who have had to defend themselves against men who wield Scripture for selfish gain.

In her letters, Francis Willard (a female preacher) confronts this same argument in 1888. Willard strongly supposes that in cases where Scripture is ineptly used in the argument against women's taking leadership in church spheres, it is a deeply self-serving case of exegetical hypocrisy. Why should such a Scripture as "I permit not women to teach . . ." be unequivocally adhered to when a similar demand, of subjection to one's older brother (found in Genesis), be aptly and largely ignored? So, it appears, as in many times past, that Scriptures are used and interpreted in the context and for the condition that the ruling class deems most fit.[84]

Willard continues that it is a "fast and loose" interpretation of Scripture that disbars women from preaching under the supposition that the text explicitly calls "men." She refutes these claims by asserting, and

---

83. Ibid., 36.
84. Frances Elizabeth Willard, *Woman in the Pulpit* (Boston: D. Lothrop Co., 1888), 20.

rightfully so, that this term "men" refers to the generalized totality of humankind and not of the specified gender. For instance, in comparison to 2 Timothy 2:2—where Paul admonishes the church to commit the things that they have heard from him to faithful men who will be able to teach others—the "men" used here in the original translation are the same "men" referred to in Acts 17:30, when God commands men everywhere to repent.[85] Is this to suppose that only men, as in males, are called to repentance? Surely not! As Christ died for all, so all are called to repentance, men and women alike.

Finally, we should look to how Jesus dealt with women, not necessarily Paul. We are Christians, followers of Christ, not of Paul; and the apostle said as much himself. Thus, it is at the example that Christ left that we look. We see Jesus' interacting with women in empowering ways throughout Scripture. He spoke with the Samaritan woman at the well. He evoked confession from Martha that He is the Christ. He protected and healed women as a part of His healing ministry. His first appearance after the Resurrection was to women. Women were present with the disciples on the day of Pentecost.

For women, they must recapture Scripture for themselves. Let the evidence speak and see that, much to the contrary, God has poured out His Spirit upon ALL flesh.[86]

In 1811, Lee married a pastor, Joseph Lee, and went with him to serve his congregation just outside the city of Philadelphia. This change for her was difficult, as she did not feel drawn to that congregation or the work that was being accomplished there. Her pleas to her husband to move back to the city were unfruitful, as he could not bear to leave his congregation behind. Through revelation of a dream, Lee soon realized that Joseph was doing the work of the Lord as he was called to do and then she was able to happily join him in ministry. This increased both her joy and the joy of her husband as they served together in the church.[87]

The next part of Lee's life was characterized by suffering. She became ill, nearly to the point of death, and suffered the loss of a number of family members over the course of just a few years. These losses also left Lee a widow, raising two children under the age of two years old. Despite these

---

85. Willard, 34.
86. See Joel 2:28.
87. Andrews, 39.

heartbreaking experiences, Lee remained steadfast in her devotion to God. While she was bedridden, she would exhort visitors who came to see her, encourage those who attended at her bedside, and commune with God in the most intimate ways.[88]

Eventually, Lee returned to her Methodist church and was officially given authority by Richard Allen to preach the Gospel. Lee's ministry was greatly evangelistic and missionary-oriented. She traveled and preached, eventually returning to her home in Cape May, New Jersey, where she held prayer meetings and revivals, which were well attended and met much success.[89]

Lee's work would also evolve to include abolitionist work with the American Antislavery Society.[90] Lee's extended autobiography was published in 1849 and little is known about her life and ministry past that point. Due to the nature of women in ministry within the Methodist Church, there are very little to no records of her participation or further involvement. This is not to say that she was not involved, but simply that the position and importance of women and their contributions were so minimized that her influences remained unrecorded and/or unrecognized.[91]

The story of Zilpha Elaw, Jarena Lee's contemporary, parallels Lee's in a number of ways. Most markedly, she was also a woman of Methodist denomination whose ministry was not cultivated within the four walls of the church. Elaw's early itinerant ministry was solely self-supported and involved her having to leave her child in the care of others after the death of her husband.[92] When Elaw was fifty years old, under the compulsion that the Spirit was driving her to go overseas, she boarded a ship and continued her evangelism throughout central England.[93] It is also interesting to note that after the time frame covered in her memoirs, very little is known about the rest of Elaw's life.

These women's writings, along with those of other contemporaries, demonstrate a number of similarities. For one, women were not apt to find opportunities to preach within congregations. Lee was encouraged to pursue exhortation, which in Methodist polity is distinctly different from

---

88. Ibid., 40.
89. Ibid., 48.
90. *Blackpast.org.*
91. Andrews, 7.
92. Ibid., 8.
93. Ibid., 8-9.

preaching. Both Lee's and Elaw's life success was largely realized through evangelism, traveling ministry, and missionary endeavors. These women had to make considerable sacrifices of family and comfort in order to live out the call they felt. While their church locales, or the men to whom they would be subordinate, did not support their ministries, they were nonetheless able to preach thousands of sermons and produce the fruit of conversion in a myriad of lives. Both of these women's narratives show a tension between faith life and domesticity and, interestingly enough, they were only able to fully bloom into ministry after their husbands passed away. This represents some of the pressures that women experienced at that time as keepers of the home who were called to outside ministry. This tension can be seen in the roles that were often delegated to women within the church, such as missionaries, hostesses, cooks, and ministerial support. They were often more the "help" than given any leadership roles.

Nevertheless, both Elaw and Lee, in their era, represent a departure from the norm—not just in the fact that they were women preachers but that they were so of their own unction, empowered by the call and inspiration of the Spirit of God. These women and their courage, opposition to status quo, and devotion to God for His purposes colored the landscape of women in ministry and set new precedents for female independence in a world of male dominance and patriarchy. They led the way for a number of women that would emerge after them, including women like Prathia Hall.

Prathia Hall

Much of Prathia Hall's life was devoted not only to God but also to community. From a young age, she was recognized for her leadership potential and was groomed as a successor for her father, a Baptist minister at Mount Sharon Baptist Church in Philadelphia.[94] Hall's father nurtured her into a theology of "Freedom Faith," which gave Hall a sense of inherent value, worth, and self-love based on nothing more than her immutable position as a child of God.[95] These theological roots would inform the rest of her life and development as she became an important figure in many civil rights circles and movements throughout the 1960s.

Hall's involvement in the Civil Rights Movement exposed her to a number of dangerous and precarious situations. When she graduated

---

94. PBS, "PEOPLE OF FAITH: Prathia Hall," *This Far by Faith* (Episode 4), 2003, http://www.pbs.org/thisfarbyfaith/people/prathia_hall.html (accessed March 1, 2017).
95. Ibid.

from Temple University, she became extensively involved in the Student Nonviolent Coordinating Committee (SNCC). Although SNCC, in the spirit of Martin Luther King Jr., espoused nonviolence, it did not spare them from being subjected to violence at the hands of others. Hall worked in some of the most violence-ridden areas of the Civil Rights Movement, including Terrell County (nicknamed "Tombstone Territory" because of the depth and severity of violence there).[96]

Hall's theology continued to be formed in the midst of the Civil Rights Movement as she recalled the intermingling of faith and social justice present in many meetings and rallies. In 1962, Hall went to Georgia to participate in the movement there. While she was working with the Albany Georgia project, every meeting was opened with prayer. Hall recalls being moved "by that power with which those songs and prayers were infused, transcended the objective reality of our situation, fashioned fear into faith, cringing into courage, suffering into survival, despair into defiance, and pain into protest."[97] She was moved by the way in which belief could transform the emotions, feelings, and even actions of individuals. Hall was confronted with White aggression, drive-by shootings at the residence where she stayed, and a number of experiences where she survived death and/or injury but others in her surroundings did not.[98]

Many have come to attribute Dr. King's famous "I Have a Dream" speech as having been inspired from a prayer prayed by Hall at one of the movement's meetings. During this prayer, Hall used the same frame of "I have a dream" that informed King's later speech, which became a grand portion of his oratorical legacy. While Hall admits remembering using the phrase, she does not recall whether King was present on that particular day.[99] Hall says that if she did inspire King, she is honored . . . and he did more with the phrase than she ever could have.[100]

Prathia endured a number of personal trials, including losing her twenty-five-year-old daughter to a stroke and being in a car accident (which gave her recurring physical issues for the rest of her life). Her battle with

---

96. SNCC Legacy Project, "Prathia Hall," Duke University, n.d., https://snccdigital.org/people/prathia-hall/ (accessed March 1, 2017).
97. Ibid..
98. PBS, "Prathia Hall," *This Far by Faith* (Episode 4).
99. D. L. Chandler, "Little Known Black History Fact: Prathia Hall," black americaweb.com. n.d. https://Blackamericaweb.com/2016/06/15/little-known-Black-history-fact-prathia-hall/ (accessed March 1, 2017).
100. Yvonne S. Lamb, "Prathia Hall: A Barrier-Breaking Woman Preacher," *Good Faith Media*, March 28, 2011, http://www.ethicsdaily.com/prathia-hall-a-barrier-breaking-woman-preacher-cms-17660 (accessed March 1, 2017).

cancer would end in her death at age 62 in 2002.[101] Nevertheless, she persevered through life's trials and proclaimed that "Faith is not faith until it is tested in the crucible of struggle and the fiery trials of life."[102] She did not shirk away from being tempted or tried, putting her life on the line, or understanding that it was not just in the glory of God to be victorious, but to suffer for faithfulness even in the face of adversity. She declared that faith is the only thing that makes things "barely bearable" and the "presence of God is really all we need."[103]

In 1965, Hall's faith and belief in the exclusive practice of nonviolent protest was shaken at a march in Selma, Alabama, which later came to be known as "Bloody Sunday." This protest march was scheduled to begin on March 7 in Selma and end in Montgomery. Six hundred marchers gathered and as they were about to cross the Edmund Pettus Bridge, they were blocked by Alabama State troopers and local police who ordered them to cease and desist. When marchers refused, police retaliated with tear gas and beatings. More than fifty people were hospitalized and many more injured. This event, and subsequent fallout, triggered the passing of the Voting Rights Act.[104] For Prathia, this event made her question her unmoving commitment to nonviolence. Looking back on this experience, Hall remarked that any nonviolent movement "has to make space for the expression of authentic anger, even rage . . . we might have had even greater power if we had somehow found a way to allow space for the expression of righteous anger."[105]

These crises ultimately drove Hall to pursue academic theology. She returned to Philadelphia to pastor her father's church and was ordained in 1977. In 1982, she became one of the first women ordained in the American Baptist Association.[106] She earned her Master of Theology and PhD in ethics, theology, and African American church history with a focus in womanist ethics from Princeton Theological Seminary. She would ultimately go on to become the Martin Luther King Jr. Chair in Social

---

101. Chandler, 1.
102. Prathia Hall, "When Faith Trembles." February 6, 2000, http://www.30goodminutes.org/index.php/archives/23-member-archives/648-prathia-hall-program-4318 (accessed February 20, 2017).
103. Ibid.
104. Jessie Kindig, "Bloody Sunday Protest March, Selma, Alabama, March 7, 1965," Blackpast.org, November 24, 2007, http://www.Blackpast.org/aah/bloody-sunday-selma-alabama-march-7-1965 (accessed February 20, 2017).
105. Ellen Cantarow, "Portrait of Prathia Hall," Medium.com, January 3, 2017, https://medium.com/@ellencantarow/ii-portrait-of-prathia-hall-63fed124049c (accessed February 20, 2017).
106. Lamb, 1.

Ethics at Boston University's School of Theology, where she taught Christian ethics and courses on the Civil Rights Movement.[107]

When asked about her experiences of self-defining herself in womanist theology and Black preaching, Hall remarked, "I stood in the authenticity of my being: Black, preacher, Baptist, woman. For the same God who made me a preacher made me a woman, and I am convinced that God was not confused on either account."[108] This declaration has echoes of both Lee and Elaw as they found their very existence to be evidence of their having been chosen by God. Lee rooted her declaration in Mary, Elaw found the truth in her ability to convert and inspire, Hall found herself at the intersection of life and legacy and was able to walk in her father's footsteps as a minister and a preacher.

In the face of controversy about women preachers, they preach, and then declare in the legacy of Sojourner Truth, "Ain't I a woman?" It should not be foreign that women, as created by God for His purposes, would be able to be unbound by the critiques and categories of man. If God can use a donkey to talk to Balaam, He certainly can use any willing mouthpiece—including women(!)—to declare His Word.

Prathia Hall's death in 2002 was not without legacy. Today, she continues to be remembered for her passionate sermons, the depth of her academic worth, her contributions to feminist and womanist thought, her influence on the Civil Rights Movement, and her fierce commitment to the call of Christ in both the social and religious spheres. Although Hall encountered a number of trying circumstances in her life, like her sisters who came before her, she nonetheless overcame, persevered, and was able to land—standing up—declaring that she would go with God. While Lee's and Elaw's legacies were up to them to write and disseminate, a change in time and attitude allowed Hall's legacy to have a different platform.

First, Hall came from a family of preachers and was able to fall into this profession through the legacy of her father. Unlike Lee, whose parents had no religious or spiritual grounding and therefore could not instruct her in her young age, Hall received a great theology grounding and legacy from her father. It was from this legacy that she was able to birth her "Freedom Faith" theology which was a hallmark of her social justice and

---
107. Cantarow, 1.
108. Yvonne S. Lamb, *My Soul Rhythms: Prayer Stories to Ignite Your Spirit* (Nashville, TN: WestBow Press, 2015), 25

professional work even later in life. It gave her a deep-rooted sense of self-worth and surety of God's love and presence in her life. She was able to cultivate these roots from an early age and turn them toward community matters, social justice issues, and eventually academic theological works centered on womanism. Her education allowed her a greater depth of influence in her later life when she would assume teaching and Chair positions at Boston University.

Second, Hall lived during a different time than both Elaw and Lee. Different resources were available to Hall, more opportunities, and the platform of the Civil Rights Movement was both an excellent springboard and a fitting backdrop for the work that she was doing. In a time of high spirituality, political unrest, the Women's Rights Movement, and visibility for Black leadership, she was able to lead and emerge on a number of fronts as a spokesperson for the movement. The intersection between church life and the Civil Rights Movement was very blurred, as churches were often the meeting places for various groups and the center of Black life and community in much of the South. This allowed for an easy marriage between church work, preaching, social justice work, and civil rights advocacy. This is one of the reasons why Martin Luther King Jr. was able to develop into the historical figure that we know him as today. He was a preacher, a pastor, and a social activist—three things that did not require any differentiation during his lifetime.

Lastly, Hall was a member of the Baptist denomination, which makes a bit of a difference when compared with Lee's and Elaw's experiences in the Methodist church. Due to the way the Methodist church is governed, even if Lee and Elaw had been able to convince their local pastors to support them in preaching, the *Discipline* (or ruling document of the church) would not allow the church to officially ordain women. This has continued to be an issue, even in recent Methodist church life, as the African Methodist Episcopal Church only elected its first female to the highest office of bishop in 2000.[109] In 2008, the African Methodist Episcopal Zion Church followed with the election of a female to the bishopric.[110]

Hall, as a member of the Baptist denomination, was a part of a different legacy for women. In 1979, there were already many women preachers

---

109. African Methodist Episcopal Church, *Tenth Episcopal District of the African Methodist Episcopal Church*, n.d, http://www.10thdistrictame.org/bishop.html (accessed February 20, 2017).
110. Melanie Tucker, "Hines elected first female bishop for AME Zion Church," *The Daily Times*, September 10, 2012.

in the Baptist denomination, although it wasn't until that year that the Baltimore District allowed them to be admitted to the conference.[111] This began the long and expedient process of women becoming a more integrated part of all Baptist church life from the pulpit to the pew.[112]

Prathia Hall was afforded a great realm of influence due to circumstances she created and some she did not create. Her life and legacy led her to be a part of the rich tapestry of women in ministry who overcame great obstacles to fight for the call on their lives . . . much like the final figure we will examine: Barbara Harris.

Barbara Harris

Barbara C. Harris was born June 12, 1930, and was the first woman to be ordained a bishop in the Anglican church.[113] Although she is currently retired, her work both within the religious community and in the broader social community have established her as a woman on the forefront for women's rights in ministry and their ability to answer the unequivocal call of God on their lives.

Harris was born and raised in Philadelphia and excelled in school life through college. Much like Hall, Harris also was a participant in the Civil Rights Movement and was even present at the Selma march ("Bloody Sunday"). The march was pivotal for both women. Harris worked in Greenville, Mississippi, registering voters. She dismissed the violence and constant threat of violence in the work that she did by declaring that "Everyone was in danger."[114] This is the courage that many participants of the Civil Rights Movement had to show; however, it also had ties to the legacy of women who chose to stand out in civil and religious life. For women, threats against their person were, in many cases, more severe—as they could suffer sexual bodily violations by their attackers that were usually not exacted on men. This heightened the threat against women and made their courage in the face of these issues even more profound.

Harris was ordained a deacon in 1979 and became a priest in 1980. In 1988, she became the interim director of the Church of the Advocate.[115] In February 1989, Harris became the first woman ordained as a bishop in the

---

111. Fitts, 310.
112. Ibid., 312.
113. Archives of the Episcopal Church, The, "The Right Reverend Barbara Harris," 2008, https://exhibits.episcopalarchives.org/s/episcopal-church-women/page/barbara-harris (accessed February 20, 2017).
114. Wikipedia, https://en.wikipedia.org/wiki/Barbara_Harris_(bishop).
115. Ibid.

Anglican church. This, coupled with her ethnicity, opened her up to be the target of harassment, death threats, and obscene messages.[116] Her ordination also caused tension between the Anglican and Catholic churches, as Catholic churches do not recognize women in the priesthood and were staunchly opposed to these changes.[117] Although the threat and danger were very real, any effort to get Harris to increase police presence, wear body armor, or otherwise take extensive measures of self-protection were denied by her. She declared that she did not take any of this backlash personally and instead rose to fight the opposition. Her response to these controversies won her respect in many circles.[118]

For Harris, she found purpose and pride in her identity not just as a woman, but as a Black woman. She declared, "I certainly don't want to be one of the boys. I want to offer my peculiar gifts as a Black woman . . . a sensitivity and an awareness that comes out of more than a passing acquaintance with oppression." Much like the women before her, she was preaching or in her position *in spite of* her being a woman. She was in it particularly because she offered value and purpose *directly because* she is a woman. In her book *Woman in the Pulpit*, Frances Elizabeth Willard further echoes this necessity of the woman preacher in a letter received from T. Dewitt Talmage. He wrote, "about the subject of women's preaching let me say that I do not think the story of the Gospel will be fully told until Christian women all around the world tell it. There is a tenderness and a pathos and a power in woman's voice, when she commends pardon and sympathy, which the masculine voice can never reach."[119]

Harris would hold the position of bishop until 2003. She retired and was succeeded by another African American woman named Gayle Elizabeth Harris.[120] In every sense, she had passed the torch of leadership to another woman who took it up and was able to continue to build on the forward progress and momentum that Harris had begun with her inauguration. While Harris' background was quite diverse, it was her writing that allowed her to be propelled to where she found success as bishop. Shortly after her ordination, she began to work for the Episcopal

---

116. Ibid.
117. African American Registry, "Barbara Harris, A Spiritual First," June 12, 2000, http://www.aaregistry.org/historic_events/view/barbara-harris-spiritual-first (accessed February 20, 2017).
118. Ibid.
119. Willard, 9.
120. M. McMickle, *An Encyclopedia of African American Christian Heritage* (Philadelphia: Judson Press, 2002), 100.

Publishing Company and write for their paper, *The Witness*.[121] Harris' skill at writing had been honed from a young age since she wrote for the school newspaper in high school.[122]

In recent work, Harris' advocacy has extended beyond women's rights and racial rights to include gay rights as well. Harris vocalized her opposition regarding the sacrament of marriage and its denial to homosexual couples. She exhorted, "What right does anyone have to draw lines beyond to whom God's grace, care and favor extend. . . . God has no favorites. Yet again, we gather at convention to debate and resolve who should and shouldn't, who can and can't receive God's blessing."[123] Her position is a liberal one and ties into her life legacy of fighting for equality for all individuals. This again has caused her to be a polarizing figure between liberal thought and more conservative Christian doctrine.[124]

The legacy of Barbara Harris tied in greatly the legacies of the women who came before. Primarily, while the platform that she emerges from is distinctly different by timeline and denomination from the other women discussed, she is nonetheless an equal partner in their courage and vision for defining and redefining roles for women. Harris continues in the legacy laid by Lee and Elaw, that perpetuates down to women such as her and Hall. They each had to define themselves outside of the current status quo and decide that they would stand up for who they believed themselves to be and who they believed God called them to be, before sitting down to patriarchy and outdated gender norms.

Much of this required a new look at Scripture and interpretation of what God was saying about men, women, and the world. If one is to believe that *"God is no respecter of persons,"*[125] this must extend to every facet of His being—including the facet that declares who shall preach His Word to His people.

Barbara Harris remains a controversial figure for some of her rhetoric; however, she is a pioneer in paving the way for women in the Episcopal church. The women all have individual stories that may have been

---

121. Ibid., 102.
122. The HistoryMakers, "Bishop Barbara Harris," February 12, 2007, http://www.thehistorymakers.com/biography/bishop-barbara-harris (accessed February 20, 2017).
123. David Virtue and Michael Heidt, "Episcopal Bishop Barbara Harris Denies Sacrament of Marriage," Catholic Online, July 16, 2009, http://www.catholic.org/news/national/story.php?id=34090 (accessed February 20, 2017).
124. Ibid.
125. Acts 10:34 (KJV)

colored by their experiences in their particular denominations; however, similarities lie within them all. For one, many of the women that achieved any level of leadership had to have support of a male clergy member. In many ways, this remains the case in contemporary church life. These women also had to make considerable sacrifice to follow the call they felt on their life. Out of loyalty to God and persistence in their worthiness, they were able to lay the groundwork for contemporary women to follow the call that God placed on their lives.

The following chapter will offer insight into the thoughts, struggles, lives, and lived theology of contemporary Black woman preachers from a number of different experiences, backgrounds, and denominations.

Chapter 3

From History to Herstory:
Black Women in Contemporary Ministry

The challenges of women in ministry are not just historical. In many ways, their journey continues even today to establish themselves as equal partners in many denominations and as equally called by God to leadership positions in the church. From the legacy of Deborah in the Old Testament to the women discussed in the preceding chapter, their stories continue to be formed and informed by the changing trends in the church.

Despite many forward strides in feminism, gender equality, and the dismantling of patriarchy in the society and the church, women continue to face considerable challenges within church leadership roles. In many ways, the church, rather than being progressive in the fight for equality, instead becomes a trickle-down reflection of the thrust of society. As such, the church continues to wrestle with issues that have found some resolution in the social sphere.

Upon interviewing modern women in ministry, their stories and testimonies continue to resemble those of their forebears. They contain the common threads of service, both inside and outside the church, finding difficulty in being endorsed by their male leaders, and often having to balance or make difficult choices between family obligations and church advancement. Despite the presence and influence of feminism on traditional gender roles in society, women are still viewed as the central caretakers of home and hearth. As such, they face challenges related to balancing work, life, and call with which many men do not have to wrestle. Women cite struggling to validate their identities as ministers in conjunction with their identities as mothers and wives. Some even opt out of the latter in order to give more time and attention to the former. As much as times have essentially changed, in many ways, they remain the same.

Much like women in history, contemporary women have found joy in Christian service despite these overwhelming odds. Women's testimonies of service, not just those interviewed directly, but other women as well, include profound experiences of joy in Christian service. Against all odds, these women not only overcame obstacles but found a way to serve with a spirit of gratitude and appreciation for all that God has allowed them to do and experience in His kingdom. This is profound—as it is a testament to the indomitable spirit of women, as well as to the faithfulness of God to produce joy out of mourning.[126]

Although challenges for women continue to persist in present-day ministries, there are a number of ways in which progress has been made and women are able to find their footing and influence in ministry. Despite these challenges, women in ministry continue to proclaim the call of God on their lives and find joy in ministry and service. This chapter will examine the nature of women called to ministry, the challenges that they face, and the joys that they experience, in spite of considerable obstacles.

Call

Women experience the call to leadership in a myriad of ways. The common thread is that many women choose to await absolute confirmation of the call to ministry before making any moves toward traditional leadership. This could be for a number of reasons.

For some women, there is a great deal at stake. Many women have responsibilities to the home and family life. A substantial sacrifice would be required with the added pressure of pastoral/ministerial leadership. It is no wonder that many women wait until they are confident and assured of their call, especially with the outside pressure that comes from the male-dominated denominations that seek to discourage them from serving in the manner and capacity in which they feel compelled by God. It is important to be completely confident in their call so that when external pressures arise they cannot be easily moved.

All women interviewed expressed equally their lack of confidence at the first moment of call. They cited that it was the testimonies and personal encouragement of other women as well as the reconfirmation of the call through encounters with God and through the course of life—including attending seminary and receiving relevant training—that led them to fulfill their call. These women were able to see God at work, not only in their spiritual lives, but in their personal and professional lives as well. They were able to directly pinpoint the contribution of sexism to much of what they have experienced in their journey toward ministerial leadership. For

---

126. See Isaiah 61:3.

some women, it has taken a male leader to take them under wing and navigate them through the murky waters of church hierarchy.

When working out their call, these women identified that they had different approaches to finding their footing in the church. One cites,

> *The pastor took me under his wing, nurturing me and giving me opportunities other women called were not being offered, simply because I submitted to leadership. I taught Sunday school. I succumbed to the missionary work in the church in visiting the sick and those in prison. I was not that one to advocate for change by resistance. I was not over-zealous and this became my manner.*
>
> *Seminary was where I experienced the triad of oppressions—sexism, classism, and inferiority. The unequal treatment of being looked over, not called upon to pray or read the Scripture. The disrespect of being the only female in a class of thirty young men; the disrespect for me as a person. These were the challenges I faced and overcame, as I have since graduated Summa Cum Laude.*[127]

She found that it was her demure attitude and submission to leadership that allowed her to move upward in ministry. She was not forceful or rebellious and instead found that tapping into her feminine traits was more effective in her carving out a place in ministry for herself than taking up the banner of protest and opposition. Of course, this has not always been the case historically nor contemporarily.

It takes a particular setting and a particular type of male leader who is already open to women in leadership in order to recognize the ministerial call of God on a woman's life to serve in a leadership capacity. This interviewee experienced fruit when she submitted to leadership because fortunately her male leader was open to her and her expressed call.

This is very similar to some of the stories of historical women in ministry who, serving in conventional mainline denominations, obtained their footing in ministry through the endorsement of the male leaders. For many, due to the climate of service, this still resulted in their having to assume positions as missionaries or act as subordinate ministers, but it nonetheless was pivotal toward their receiving any recognition as leaders at all.

---

127. Interview with a Minister, February 2016.

While male endorsement has been helpful in some cases, it has not always been possible, and women have had to discover or create their own ministerial niches. Such was the case with many of the women firsts in ministry and continues to be the case with contemporary women in ministry. Women confronted with patriarchal opposition must persevere "in spite of" and even, sometimes, carve out a niche for themselves outside of the church or conventional church roles.

While church leadership and society may discount women in ministry, it is often the very ones that society counts out that God opts to use for His purposes. The biblical record has a legacy of displaying God's selection of underdogs and "the least" of society to do His work. David was the youngest, and a shepherd boy. Ruth was a widow. Esther was a young Jewish girl. Hagar was an outcast from her family. Jesus continues this legacy in selecting the twelve disciples from the lower rungs of society. He selected fishermen, tax collectors, and working-class men to follow Him and be His closest friends and confidantes.[128] Likewise, then, it should come as no surprise that God would choose to use women, the disadvantaged, and socially oppressed, to spread His Gospel. Black women, even more so. It remains that God calls and uses whom He will, how He chooses, and our estimation of right and wrong has no bearing on God's selection. This is a wonderful testimony to the legacy of women in history and the potential of women to serve in the future. Certainly, *"the last shall be first."*[129]

Renita Reems—preacher, scholar, and author in the A.M.E. Zion church—describes her call as feeling something "pulling me, drawing me, urging me on . . . ." While it is customary in the Methodist tradition to describe a distinct "call," Reems also acknowledges that once she lived into that call, she found that in the church tradition, her gifts made room for her.[130] She was uniquely suited for work in the ministry and what that entailed through her life experiences.[131]

More women experience this dynamic as well, especially as leadership styles within the church continue to shift. Women find their life experiences and characteristics as nurturers, home managers, and encouragers are more acceptable as leadership traits in modern church dynamics.[132]

---

128. Ella Mitchell, *Women: To Preach or Not to Preach: 21 Outstanding Black Preachers Say Yes!* (Pennsylvania: Judson Press, 1991), 38.
129. Matthew 20:16 (KJV).
130. See Proverbs 18:16.
131. Maureen Fiedler, *Breaking Through the Stained Glass Ceiling: Women Religious Leaders in Their Own Words* (New York: Seabury Books, 2010), 137.
132. McKenzie, 62.

Unlike men, whose success is often their own, women find that their fruit and their call is often more communal in nature. For one thing, as staples in the home, especially with more single-parent homes, the call on a women's life directly affects others—including husbands, dependents, and/or children. In addition, women's ministries are often more interconnected than men's, especially due to the nature of oppression they have historically experienced.

On the advent of her election as the first female bishop in the African Methodist Episcopal Church, Vashti Mckenzie recalls being told by Bishop H. H. Brookins, "If you fail, it will be a long time before another woman will have this opportunity. But if you succeed, it'll never be your success, it will always be someone else's."[133] This is the legacy of women in church service: their failure is their own and can often bar the way for other women. Their success likewise is not theirs but can also represent the success and progression of a community. In this way, the call on a woman's life is never hers alone, but has an outward reaching and trickle effect with deep roots into all the communities of which she is a part. Many times, men do not have these same considerations as they live out the call of God on their lives. They are afforded leeway and ownership of their actions without its being placed on the entire community of male leadership.

Challenges

Womanism theology is the point of departure of Black women's theological thought. It is the branch of theology that uniquely identifies the struggles of Black women as an intersection of sexism, classism, and racism that is unique to the experience of Black women in America.[134] This is significant because, to many, racism was inherent in their writings and interactions with Black women and why womanism had to develop separate from the feminist movement. Bell Hooks writes,

> *Racism abounds in the writings of white feminists, reinforcing white supremacy and negating the possibility that women will bond politically across ethnic and racial boundaries. Past feminist refusal to draw attention to and attack racial hierarchy suppressed the link between race and class. Yet class*

---

133. Fiedler, 14.
134. Jacqueline Grant, "Womanist Theology: Black Women's Experience as a Source for Doing Theology," in *Sisters Struggling in the Spirit*, N. B. Lewis et al. (Louisville: Presbyterian Church, 1994), 18.

structure in American society has been shaped by the racial politic of white supremacy.[135]

So, there is contention between White women and Black women in ministry because of an inability and unwillingness for White women, both historically and contemporarily, to relate to the unique struggles of Black women and their (White women) complicity in those conditions.

Even after working out their personal call and the compulsion to serve God in formal leadership capacities, often requiring confronting and overcoming significant internal struggles, women in leadership in the church face considerable other challenges. The first place that women have to confront challenges is often in their own families. Opposition from males in their families, including uncles and fathers, was/is not uncommon. Interestingly, some women spoke out against other women family members assuming pastoral leadership in the church. Some of the dissenting women felt as if women assuming these positions would be forced to place loyalty and time with their families in competition with their work within the church.[136] For many women, however, confronting these attitudes within their families and standing firm about their call in the face of opposition laid the groundwork for doing the same within the context of the church itself. The women interviewed were able to cite overcoming these direct challenges as a major part of the confidence they gained in the ministry regarding the surety of their call and service.

One interviewee established that it was demonstrative of the work and power of God through her and in her work when a male parishioner, who was outspoken and adamant about his refusal to accept women in leadership, later experienced a profound move of God due to a word that she preached. This further solidified to her, and also to him, that God is able to supersede all boundaries of race, class, gender, and status to achieve His necessary work.[137] This is a valuable lesson in the lives of all young ministers, both male and female—namely that God can use you in spite of what can be perceived as insufficiencies or failings on our own part.

This opposition from males, both in the church and in the community, has been an ongoing issue for women in ministry. As discussed in previous chapters, the social and political climate of various eras certainly

---

135. Bell Hooks, *Feminist Theory: From Margin to Center* (Boston: South End Press, 1984), 3.
136. Minister Interview 2, February 2017.
137. Minister Interview 2, February 2017.

contributed to the pressure that men exerted to maintain dominion and power in the church. Where many men already felt oppressed by society, church became the realm where they could exert their power and purpose without being suppressed. This caused tension when women tried to infiltrate the ranks of leadership.[138]

Although some would argue that the social pressures of Jim Crow no longer exist, there is still a struggle for power in the lives of Black men as many still feel disenfranchised. Having an exclusive sphere of influence like the church is an important part of the identity of some vested Black men. It was not just sexism but also social pressure that caused such a rift between sexes in the clergy. The idea that the language of the Bible is entrenched in male-gendered pronouns—coupled with the reality that Jesus is a man—creates a psychological rift for many regarding the presence of women in ministry.

And, much like historic women, contemporary Black women have to combat perceptions of their bodies. This is a familiar struggle that continues to persist today. One interviewee writes,

> One of the things that concerns me, though I am not sure if it is an insecurity, is the perception of some men in the ministry who want to reduce me to a "skirt" because I choose to be not only a woman in ministry but a lady. The treatment is often condescending and it causes me to display a less than warm temperament in some situations and to uncomfortably laugh off other situations as harmless, even when they do not feel harmless. I also find that I feel I must constantly keep my emotions in check because of the perception.[139]

Women have struggled to assimilate the feminine into their ministries without creating an atmosphere where their credibility or service is questioned and critiqued unnecessarily. Historically, the feminine has always challenged the predominantly male-leaning profession of clergy. Nonetheless, although many women feel this pressure, there is a modern movement, closely tied to the rebirth of feminism, where women have rejected the idea that they have to be either/or and instead opt to be both. They hold the tension of the feminine and the godly in contention with

---

138. R. Marie Griffith and Barbara Dianne Savage, eds., *Women and Religion in the African Diaspora: Knowledge, Power, and Performance* (Baltimore, Maryland: John Hopkins University Press, 2006), 143.
139. Minister Interview, February 2017.

one another and work out what it means to be both in the context of religious service.[140] This can be especially challenging depending on the denomination. Pentecostal and nondenominational churches are more open to these changes whereas more mainline and conservative denominations are more reluctant to accept these changes and dichotomies.

There continues to be a stigma of women, particularly emphasized when Vice President Mike Pence, a known evangelical, admitted that he does not sit down to a meal alone with another woman, nor does he consume alcohol, without his wife present.[141] This sets up a dynamic that women are inherently untrustworthy and a risky gamble. Attitudes like this make it difficult for women to develop mentorship relationships that otherwise might help them to progress in ministry.

This attitude toward men's interacting with women in solitary settings is referred to as the "Billy Graham Rule," as it was popular televangelist Billy Graham that offered his public support of the practice.[142] This rule is often used by Protestant Christian leaders where they avoid spending time alone with women who are not their wives. The idea is that this practice minimizes the risk of temptation and infidelity. Unfortunately, what this also does is create a culture where women are inherently vilified and looked at as temptresses, seductresses, and vixens, even if no such relationship or intention exists on their behalf. This belief system has led to interesting rules and interactions between male leaders and females within congregations where women are often only allowed to interact with other women or encouraged to seek out other spiritual mentorship when males are in charge. This creates an atmosphere that makes it difficult for women to excel and rise through the hierarchy in the same way as men, especially if the very men who openly avoid deep interaction with them are the ones who would have to endorse their fitness for ministry.

An additional challenge, similar to the male perception problem but also much deeper, is the challenge that certain biblical interpretations lend to the idea of women in ministry. For decades, women in ministry were perceived as being forbidden due to some of the New Testament writings of Paul and women's lack of mention (mostly in the Old Testament), in leadership roles save for a few instances. The idea that forbidding the participation of women in certain ranks of ministry due to biblical wording and

---
140. Minister Interview, February 2017.
141. Bob Allen, "The 'Billy Graham Rule' and Women in Ministry," in *Baptist News Global*, 6 April 2017: 1.
142. Ibid.

interpretation is the backbone of the male issue and sexism in ministry. Without these seemingly "supportive" Scriptures, much of the rhetoric espoused would have no grounding; however, that is not the case.

Womanist theology begins with the experience of God and is founded and grounded in the biblical text; however, reading one's identity into the text sometimes requires a reinterpretation of the text. Jacqueline Grant asserts that "to do Womanist theology we must read and hear the Bible and engage it within the context of our own experience."[143] This is also reflected in the experience of renowned liberation theologian Howard Thurman, who recalls an experience with his grandmother, who vowed, if she ever learned to read, that she would skip the part of the Bible cited by slave masters to control slaves where Paul admonishes obedience to masters.[144] We see here a practice of accepting the liberation of the text over the oppression of the biblical text with intention and resolve.[145]

Some of these other oppressive texts also include Paul's admonishing women to keep silent in the congregation and the open reference to elders and deacons in the church as men (exclusively) have been reclaimed by modern leading women in thought and practice. These women instead point to the empowering stories of women in the biblical text who obviously served God in many capacities, including Hagar, Deborah, and Anna.

Women have not only faced obstacles in becoming part of church leadership but quite specifically in their service as pastors, the chief of all leaders in the church. The role of the pastor is one that encompasses a variety of roles encompassing all aspects of congregants' lives. This would include providing religious, spiritual, social, emotional, etc., guidance; ceremony leadership for family care, weddings, funerals, and so on; and, of course, weekly sermons and services.

Biblically, followers of Christ were disciples (students) or apostles who were selected to represent Him. However, the minister's role goes far beyond that. A minister is expected to be the following:

1. A person of deep faith developed through an intimate relationship with Him;
2. A proclaimer of the Gospel, in conventional settings often through the written and the spoken Word, in the pulpit and in other mediums;

---
143. Grant, 187.
144. Grant, 186.
145. Ibid.

3. A servant, both of others and the church. In Baptist tradition, this often extends to being an active agent of social justice and change in the community;

4. A steward who provides the community and congregation they serve with guidance, correction, strength, and edification;

5. In large, the minister is a vessel through which the Lord works.[146]

If being a minister were an ordinary job description, this would be a tall order for anyone to fill. Likely, not many would rise to this employment opportunity. However, ministers often have to exemplify all of these qualities as well as many more. They often have to act as counselors for members of their congregation, confidantes, community liaisons, educators, etc. In addition to being spiritual leaders, many pastors sometimes have secular jobs as well. In light of this, women face considerable challenges.

First, there is a lack of women role models. It is much easier to contextualize and visualize a role if one has the opportunity to observe and interact with others who have been on a similar life path. There is a dearth of women in leadership roles and often they are put in competition with one another instead of positioned to assist one another. Many women feel as if they must compete for "the woman's spot" in any ministry and therefore cannot foster a spirit of sisterhood easily.[147]

Nevertheless, the dynamic of women in leadership has been shifting in recent years as women's empowerment and presence in leadership has penetrated. While historically, leadership was characterized by traits that were more exemplified by males, contemporary leadership models have shifted more toward traits that are characterized as feminine.[148]

> *Women leaders, generally speaking, encourage participation, share power and information, enhance other people's self-worth, get others excited about their work, solicit input, create positive environments, and empower others.*[149]

As leadership models continue to shift, and church models change to transformative models, women find themselves more easily able to mold

---
146. McKenzie, 63.
147. Ibid., 67.
148. Ibid., 70.
149. Ibid., 71.

leadership positions and be accepted. For many younger women in ministry, the opportunity to serve is not something they waited on to arrive; instead, they adopted the attitude that they should "Just do it." They looked at rejection as opportunity to do something else and preferred to be self-reliant if they found that no one was interested in offering assistance or support for their endeavors.[150] Unfortunately, the church has not been a beacon of light leading the way for women in leadership but has, instead, been pulled along by the tide of secular society.[151]

Many acknowledge the deep double standard that exists for women in ministry that makes it nearly impossible to navigate identity in clergy-hood. In her book *Not Without a Struggle*, Vashti McKenzie elaborates thusly:

> . . . *if a clergywoman is too good looking she is regarded suspiciously by other women and men. If she is committed to her ministry, then she must be unhappy at home. If she balances her work and home life, then she is neglecting her "call." If she looks too glamorous, then she is looking for extra male companionship. If she does not look at all glamorous, then she has no self-pride. If she dresses too well or lives too "high on the hog," then she must be stealing. If she does not live well enough, she is an embarrassment to God and the church. If she is single, then she must be scouting the congregation for a husband. If she is a married woman, she must either be playing the field or not taking care of her husband or children properly.*[152]

With all of these pressures and scrutiny placed upon every action, women have to tread lightly and intentionally when making decisions in ministry. Men generally do not face the same scrutiny and pressure. McKenzie continues,

> *Male leaders' mistakes may be overlooked, forgiven or subject to appropriate reprimands. Female leaders' mistakes may receive the same treatment, but the women interviewed indicated that a mistake could be like a "sickness unto death" for them in local churches or denominational organizations. Some clergymen's indiscretions may be overlooked and/or*

---

150. Ibid., 83.
151. Fiedler, 102.
152. McKenzie, 85.

> *forgiven. But clergywomen's indiscretions brand them, even taint their reputations, for a long time; they may become a hole from which it is difficult to climb out. The gossip about the same slips in judgment seems juicier and to travel farther when a female leader is involved.*[153]

Joys

For many women, despite the challenges they face and hurdles they have to leap over or around, they are still able to find deep joy in serving God. From way back to current days, women, explaining the joy that they derive from ministry, state that they are content to know that they are doing the will of God. Despite the challenges and issues or delays with accepting their call, they nonetheless find their deepest joy in the assurance that they are living out their lives in the way God intended.

This is no small notion and bespeaks the depth of faith and love for service that is found in the hearts of women that are chosen by God. For women choosing religious leadership, there are many more compromises than there are for men. Traditionally, women have had the responsibility of raising children and caring for the home, and they may not be able to fully commit themselves to those roles exclusively. Additionally, women, unlike most men, oftentimes fight not only internal demons of self-doubt but also counteract the opposition that the world, both inside and outside of the church, continues to volley at them.

There are countless biblical stories and stories of contemporary women in ministry who have found their ultimate joy within the will of God. Like many biblical women, it wasn't the extraordinary nature of their lives that set them apart, but their being set apart that caused them to be extraordinary.

Take, for instance, some of the prominent women of the Bible:

- **Mary**, mother of Jesus: Relatively speaking, she was a regular young woman from an obscure town. She is not remarkable by worldly standards due to lineage or social caste—in fact, much the opposite. Nonetheless, it was her special selection for a God-ordained task that allowed her to gain renown and distinction.
- **Deborah:** Marked in the Old Testament as a judge and prophetess, Deborah was married to Lappidoth, and she led Israel alongside

---

153. Ibid., 85

Barak; they partnered in Israel's deliverance. However, it isn't her station that affords her distinction but the fact that she allowed God to use her—bravely and mightily—in bringing about His word.

- **Rahab:** By all accounts, Rahab was a harlot, lower caste of society, and not a woman of distinction or renown. However, it is her participation in the ultimate capture of the Promised Land—a move within the will of God—that allowed her position and honor in the Old Testament and positioned her to be a part of Jesus' bloodline.
- **Anna:** By all accounts, Anna would not have been considered special. She was a widow for decades longer than she was married and had devoted herself to serving in the temple. However, it was her devotion and her simple life that allowed her to be uniquely positioned to witness the introduction of the Messiah to the world and to mark His arrival with exclamation.
- **Hannah:** Although Hannah was barren—a great disadvantage in biblical times—her patience, persistence, and faithfulness allowed her to become a marked part of the tapestry of the Old Testament. It was her devotion to God and the depth of commitment to keeping her word that set her apart.

There is no dearth of examples in both the Old and New Testaments of women mentioned that were not remarkable by social standards but were great because of the power of God at work in their lives and how they surrendered to that power. Women in ministry today cite these same sentiments, and, in fact, ministry can be a place of great power and identity for women. Women that feel powerless or voiceless in various other spheres can find identity and purpose in entering the ministry and serving the will of God.

Minister Renita Reems discusses her joy at creating a platform for women to reclaim their power in ministry by fully possessing their womanist voice and tapping into their intuition.[154] It is important to find God even in the silence and in the doubt. In fact, this is part of the Christian life—fall down seven times, get up eight.[155]

The faith of women has continuously been tested. It is in the continued faithfulness to God that conviction is built and deepened. In this way,

---
154. Fiedler, 134.
155. Ibid., 135.

even the considerable struggles of women are a blessing in disguise for their interior faith life. As women recount times when they were left out or counted out by their male peers and, yet, God still showed up, these experiences have worked to strengthen their resolve and confidence in their own ministry.

Although it is considerably long, it is worth sharing the story of one minister's visit to a church at the invitation of the pastor. She recounts, "I was invited to preach for a women's day afternoon service. When the other male ministers were escorted to the pastor's office, I was taken to a seat in the secretary's office. The usual courtesies extended to visiting preachers were not given."

She continues that she was made to sit on the front pew instead of in the pulpit and she was not allowed to enter the pulpit even to preach. She was directed to a lectern. People made comments but she says, "I ignored the comments and preached anyway." She knew that God would fight her battle for her. She writes, "People shouted and cried during the sermon, and many people came forward responding to the call for Christian discipleship. The pastor sat amazed in silence."[156]

This is just one story of how women have had to endure underhandedness and even disrespect by pastors and congregations—not only ones that they serve but also ones they are invited to serve as well. It takes fortitude and character to withstand this treatment, particularly if it is the norm instead of the exception. However, the payoff is joy! Joy to know that whom God qualifies, no one is able to disqualify! Joy that God is still able to fight battles on our behalf! Joy that God has the final say! Joy that God is faithful and will never forsake us! There is the joy of knowing that even when man would discredit and disrespect at times, God is still able to elevate and prosper one through his or her attention to His will and His purpose. Just as our historic sisters experienced such adversity, women today are still experiencing sexism and racism in the ranks of the clergy. Nonetheless, they continue to fight the good fight of faith that allows them to continue even in the midst of opposition.

One woman details that in order to fulfill the call she felt on her life she had to leave her native Baptist denomination and join the Church of Christ. Coupled with this, she notes that her greatest fear is that she will

---

156. McKenzie, 89.

not be able to be an influence in the denomination that means so much to her from her childhood. It is her hope that she could encourage other women in the ministry, but it is unfortunate that her native church would not allow her the capacity to exercise her gifts and her call.

This is a common practice nowadays where women are more educated and professionally mobile. Those who feel called to leadership, ministry, and preaching will find denominations where they are accepted and affirmed instead of battling more traditional institutions for a seat at the table.

Social media is contributing to this trend. One no longer explicitly needs a pulpit to develop a following or to use as a platform. There are many self-named evangelists, apostles, and preachers whose sphere of influence is created through their online persona. This is also a plus as they are able to reach many more individuals through social media. Facebook, Instagram, YouTube, and Twitter are growing platforms of communication. Religious mediums are no different. Women can be found creating their own platforms in their own time and making their own networks through blogging and e-conferencing.

Women are no longer serving at the whimsy of their male colleagues who refuse to see the gifts that God has placed within them. Women are no longer confined to a church with four walls. There are women in clergy who have been at both ends of the spectrum—from completely barred from pulpit ministry to fully supported and embraced by their leaders and the congregations they serve. With the proliferation of denominations and the myriad ways to do ministry available to the contemporary minister, there is no excuse to not preach the Word.

Naturally, there are those women who feel compelled to remain in denominations and in churches that suppress and/or disregard their gifts. These women choose to make the effort to remain and speak the voice that pushes for change amidst a complacent and accepting male-dominant mass. These women are pioneers in their own right.

In the words of Martin Luther King Jr., "Injustice anywhere is a threat to justice everywhere." This could be said for the oppression and seclusion that women in ministry face. As long as niches remain where women are barred from living out the call on their lives, the church, as the body of Christ, still has work to do. This is not only doing a disservice to the women whose gifts are being squelched, but it is also doing a disservice to all of the souls and lives that could be reached and saved through a Word that could only come from one of God's great women vessels.

Despite the struggles that women in general have faced in the church and in leadership capacities in the church, there are uplifting stories of journeys in denominational leadership that have been faith-growing and identity-affirming. It is through the surmounting of the obstacles in their path that they are able to find God more deeply, serve their communities more fully, and discover resiliency and resolve that they had not tapped into in any other parts of their lives.

The Black church has accepted and proliferated the oppression of Black women within their midst. This is partially due to the permeating nature of racial issues in America and the universal effect of White hegemony on masses—both the minds of the oppressed and the oppressor. These mindsets have trickled into the Black church and become a building block within their foundation. However, if the Black church is indeed going to stand for liberation, it must stand for the liberation of all in their midst and not just some. This includes working toward the true liberation and freedom from oppression of all women in their midst.

The legacy of women in Christian service is deep and varied through the history of the church. Women are an integral part of church life and a necessary aspect of the success of many ministries. Women have been missionaries, community servants, prayer warriors, preachers, teachers, and pastors. They have worked, bled, and sweated under the blood-stained banner of Christ while holding firm to their faith and all that God has compelled them to be, even in the midst of a world and a church that often only offers a resounding "No" in response to their acknowledged call of God on their lives. Even through all of this they find joy in ministry and a deeper sense of purpose and a resolve to serve no matter what. This is a testament to the spirit of a woman—and why wouldn't God want to enlist such a soul for His service? Women embody the collective attitude of Christian maturity in that they are called to endure like good soldiers. These women not only endured but also found joy in the work that they were doing. They were able to find hope, not just for themselves, but for the effectiveness of the work that they were doing. They were able to meet the challenges of their day while offering encouraging words of life to others who were facing their own unique challenges.

Many of these women exemplified grace under fire and courage in the midst of adversity. They left a legacy not only of fortitude but of grace, joy, hope, and perseverance. As this realm of ministry continues to advance, many other women can borrow strength from their stories of triumph and endurance. It is hopeful that the future church will embrace all of our myriad differences and realize that women especially have always significantly contributed to the prosperity of the Gospel and should be given leeway and authority to continue to do so.

Chapter 4

Future Role of Women in Ministry as a Catalyst for the Black Church Survival

Being Led by the Spirit

In looking at the future of the role of women in the church of the twenty-first century we have explored the history of the issue, women in ministry in their various context, and we will end this paper with the importance of the Holy Spirit, the responsibility of men, and the agency of women to advance women in ministry of the twenty-first century.

The issue that lies ahead with women in the ministry within the church is rooted in a lack of reliance of the Holy Spirit and a strong reliance on our own biased desires. Refusing to acknowledge the call of women in any ministry for God is an indictment on our understanding of biblical and spiritual things. It is through the working of the Holy Spirit that these things are revealed to us to show us a more perfect way—as Paul talks about in 1 Corinthians 12:31.

If we are going to embrace these spiritual things that push us toward a more Christ-centered view on ministry, that is opening and embracing of diversity and multifaceted aspects of Christ's redemption on the earth, we are going to have to unplug from the world and plug into the Word. The Word moves us toward this working of the Spirit that calls and equips women toward ministry. In the world in which we currently live, to be spiritually disciplined requires that one be able to get away from the activities of what is considered normal everyday life.

Spiritual discipline requires sanctification, and it seems to be that in the twenty-first century, believers are joining the ranks of nonbelievers and not wanting to be set apart for the use and the kingdom of God. In this we struggle to find room and grace to embrace how God's Spirit is working in the lives of those whom we have "othered." In doing so we now limit the Spirit and we conjure up peculiar theology that limits God and advances our own points of view.

From my involvement in the Black church, it appears that we want church membership over Christian discipleship. It appears we want to limit our interaction with Christ to an hour-and-a-half shouting fest on Sunday morning, over-and-above experiencing God and His Spirit manifesting itself through us and showing us new revelations of the Word that push us toward justice. By and large, it has been my experience that we do not want to engage Christ through spiritual sacrifices and disciplines.

In his book *Celebration of Discipline,* Richard Foster highlights these points to show us that by handcuffing the Spirit of God because of our lack of engagement in spiritual discipline, we have, in fact, limited an unlimited God in our own lives. Foster argues that we are at this proverbial point in Christendom because "we simply do not know how to go about exploring the inward life."[157]

I agree with this statement by Foster and ask the question, how have we gotten to this point of the faith when throughout the sacred text, we are reminded of the spiritual things that we need to do to make it in this world?"

The issue, as I see it, is that we have gotten away from the foundational pillars of our faith rooted in Christian spirituality. While we love spouting Pauline doctrine around the women-in-ministry-issue, we seem to forget how Paul lauded several women (whom we will get to later in the book) for their work of ministry within the church. Some of these women even led their own churches.

Foster seeks to use his text to push Christians back into a relationship with Christ. This requires us to move beyond "will power" to an authentic relationship with God through Jesus Christ, who is able to help us overcome the sins in our lives with which we are struggling. I want to be clear in my interpretation of Foster . . . I do believe that failing to acknowledge women in ministry is a sin and that we have to address this sin if we are going to move forward with ministry in the twenty-first century. If we are simply relying on our own will to do it, we will fail every time. Will power, while a good virtue toward perseverance, is not what we as people of faith rely on to push us toward Christ. It is the Holy Spirit that pushes us away from sin and sinfulness and toward Christ. In this, for me, the argument is

---

157. Richard J. Foster, *Celebration of Discipline: The Path to Spiritual Growth* (New York: HarperCollins, 2018; first published 1978), 3.

constructed about advancing women. It will not be because of will power, but because of God's power.

I agree with Foster when he states, "Willpower will never succeed in dealing with the deeply ingrained habits of sin. . . . 'Will worship' may produce an outward show of success for a time, but in the cracks and crevices of our lives our deep inner condition will eventually be revealed."[158] The human will, I argue, is rooted to the human heart. Jeremiah 17:9 reminds us that above all else, the heart is deceitful. To address this issue of the future role of women, we have to address the heart of men and women that places us here and seek God for the heart transplant that says, "He will give us in Ezekiel 36 as he renews our spirit."

We "will" things because we "heart" things; we have passion for things and that passion is rooted in our hearts. I am reminded that the heart is evil and corrupt,[159] and since the heart is evil and corrupt those things that come from the heart, even in their purest forms, are equally wicked. The will is not that which will be able to work out our salvation *"with fear and trembling"*[160] as Paul told the church at Philippi, but a true relationship is needed with God to observe these spiritual practices. It is the Spirit and spiritual practices and disciplines that are going to transform the hearts of men—to open our eyes to the way we have been treating women in the ministry and in the world.

One's relationship with Christ coupled with active spiritual discipline will enable them to overcome the sins that may be besetting them and the spiritual warfare that believers face. Foster says, "God has given us the Discipline of the spiritual life as a means of receiving his grace. The disciplines allow us to place ourselves before God so that he can transform us"[161] At the threshold of His martyrdom, Jesus prepared His followers for His impending death, much to the chagrin of the disciples. Jesus realized that He was leaving the disciples in this world to have to deal with a corrupt government that did not understand their mission and ministry and to have to deal with an equally corrupt church. According to Jesus, these people do not know God or Him, and they believe what they are doing is right. But Jesus does not leave the disciples alone; He leaves them with the gift of the Holy Spirit.[162]

---

158. Ibid., 5.
159. See Jeremiah 17:9.
160. Philippians 2:12 (NIV)
161. Foster, 7.
162. See John 16:1-7.

The "Holy Spirit" in Greek is the *paraclete* and is literally translated as "the Helper." Jesus left with us a Helper. He said that when the Holy Spirit comes He will reprove the world of sin, righteousness, and judgment, and that the Spirit is truth. The Spirit will guide believers in the truth and will not speak of His own accord—but will speak of the things that He hears and will show them things to come.[163]

To move beyond the superficial aspects of religion and to be able to transcend into a deeper relationship with God that is embracing of a transgender faith (I will unpack this later in the text), we must be willing to free ourselves of our own will and be open to the move and the will of God through the Holy Spirit. The inward disciplines and outward disciplines of meditation, prayer, fasting, studying, simplicity, solitude, submission, and service can only come to fruition when one sees these practices as a way of life to get one closer to the divine through meaningful relationship. The Holy Spirit is what God has given unto us so that we can work out our relationship in fear and trembling through these spiritual practices.

In Mark 9, a man whose son was possessed brought him to Jesus' disciples seeking that he might be healed, and the disciples could not do it. The young man was healed by Jesus. The people were in awe but the disciples were baffled. Two of them had just seen Jesus transfigured on the mountain and just days before they had seen Him feed five thousand with five loaves of bread and two small fish. They had seen Jesus perform miracles, and He had even empowered them to perform miracles—yet in this instance they failed miserably at the task at hand.

Jesus told them that these spirits only come out through fasting and praying. The disciples could not fully understand the power of these two spiritual practices. They thought that they could simply speak and the words spoken were sufficient enough for healing. Jesus had to remind them that even when you walk with God, literally, there are some things that cannot happen in the spiritual realm without first being prepared through spiritual practices.

One's surrendering oneself to the move of God becomes a pillar of spiritual discipline. Jesus says that those who will be His followers must first deny themselves and take up their crosses—then they can follow Him.[164] Throughout his epistles Paul speaks about surrendering and submission

---
163. See John 16:8-13.
164. See Mark 8:34.

to God. In Romans 12:1, he says, *"present your bodies as a living sacrifice"* (NRSVUE). In 1 Corinthians 6:18-20, he says, *"Flee from sexual sins done in the body, don't you know that your body is the temple for the Holy Spirit and that you have been brought with a price?"* (paraphrased).

One's surrendering of oneself is imperative in moving beyond being a church member to being a Christian disciple (through spiritual practices). Foster's position is that submission is freedom—and our letting go of our own desires for the desires of God is key to understanding submission. He says, "In submission we are at last free to value other people. Their dreams and plans become important to us. We have entered into a new, wonderful, glorious freedom—the freedom to give up our own rights for the good of others."[165]

Surrendering is as important in our spiritual lives as the practices themselves. To move from membership to discipleship to worship, we must live a life that is Spirit-led and constantly seeking to be renewed, rejuvenated, and revived by the Holy Spirit that lives within us.

I tend to agree with a son of the Black church who embraced the call of women. The pastor, mystic, and theologian Rev. Dr. Howard Thurman says in his book *Disciplines of the Spirit*,

> *In Christianity, there is ever the central, inescapable demand of surrender. The assumption is that this is well within the power of the individual. If power is lacking, every effort must be put forth to find out what the hindrance is. No exception is permissible.... Whatever stands in the way of the complete and full surrender, we must search it out and remove it.*[166]

This is our push, as believers in the church of the twenty-first century, to cling to the Spirit and not to flesh. We have become like the disciples who simply thought that walking with Jesus was enough. In the words of the youth of the church of today, "there is levels to this." Walking with Jesus was the first level for the disciples. Jesus was preparing them to do so much more even after He was no longer living (see John 14:12). Jesus advanced women in His ministry by refusing to condemn a woman caught in adultery (see John 8); by elevating Mary Magdalene as the first commissioned woman to carry the Gospel (see John 20); and by befriending Mary and Martha, who prospered in a patriarchal society (see John 12). It is through the Spirit that we, as men and women, are called to do greater

---

165. Foster, 112.
166. Howard Thurman, *Disciplines of the Spirit* (New York: Harper & Row, 1963), 19.

works, and in the context of this writing those greater works include men and women.

The Responsibility of Men

Without women, where would the Black church be throughout the ages?

We have already focused on the history of women within the Black church. Now we look toward a synthesis to answer the question, where do women fit in the context of the modern Black church?

Finlay notes that the nineteenth century saw a dramatic increase in the activities of women in Protestant churches and in social activism. As women became more active in their own organizations over the course of the nineteenth century, the possibility of women's ordination to official church ministry came to be discussed.[167]

Ministry is fluid and can take on many forms. As noted historically within the Black church women have been "pigeonholed" to believe that their call to the ministry was nothing more than a call to teach Sunday school, to work with youth, or a call to the mission field . . . but never a call to preach the Gospel—because, of course, that was a man's job. At the onset let me clarify that a call to teach Sunday school, to work with youth, or to serve in the mission field is not small or irrelevant to the overall gifting of ministry; however, it is not as honored and respected within the Black church as the call to preach the Gospel.

Black women make up more than 80 percent of the constituents of local Black churches, but in 2017 they made up less than a quarter of pastors in historical Black mainline denominations.[168] Ministry has been considered a *"good old boys club"* for centuries, but now, with the rise of women who are refusing to accept a hegemonic and sexist theology that relegates their gifts to the kitchen or to the Sunday school, that once elite boys club is now facing a crisis.

The acceptance of women to ministry in most Black denominations has been slow as a result of how we, as ministers, were trained by our White co-laborers in the Gospel in the eighteenth, nineteenth, and twentieth centuries.

---

167. Barbara Finlay, *Facing the Stained Glass Ceiling: Gender in a Protestant Seminary* (Maryland: University Press of America, 2002), 1.
168. Ashley Emmert, "The State of Female Pastors," in *Women Leaders*, October 15, 2015, https://www.christianitytoday.com/women-leaders/2015/october/state-of-female-pastors.html.

Black men in ministry have historically been trained to be biblical literalists. While White men have had the opportunity and the privilege to acquire learning and various modes of training to advance their theological positions, within the Black church, Black pastors are still lagging behind in receiving formal education (which I would argue is an aid to showing new perspective and learning new ideas).

While most, if not all, mainline White denominations that trained Blacks for ministry have accepted the call of women in the ministry, historical Black denominations (except for a few) have not embraced this move. Finlay notes that even in the White denomination there was a struggle for women to find a place in the preached ministry. Finlay states,

> *The pace of women's movement into leadership positions varied to some extent according to the polity of the denominations [that] were able to move quickly from women's lay leadership to accepting women as clergy, since they did not have to gain the approval of a broader organization in order to call a woman as a minister. More hierarchical denominations, including Presbyterians, were slower to ordain women, since this type of change had to be approved by the higher authority structures before local congregations could act. Zikmuud points out that even women's lay leadership required greater theological rationale in these churches. She further notes that, once these churches agreed to the theological permissibility of women's ordination they still resisted its implementation for many decades by appealing to a variety of pragmatic concerns.*[169]

Once women were accepted (I use that word intentionally in place of the word "allowed") in the ministry, their very way of being as preacher and pastor proved to be different than men have historically pastored.

With a woman in the preached ministry the conversation about compensation and benefits alone has changed. For example, when men pastor, usually there is no conversation about paternity leave in the context of most local churches. With women pastoring this is a conversation that must be had.

How women and men interact with the local church is unique to their own gender. The way women and men even interact in ministry proves

---

169. Ibid., 2.

to be different. Finlay says that there is a growing body of evidence that certain differences in fact do exist in the behavior and attitudes of male and female clergy, even though it would seem that ministerial vocations in general would lean toward the more stereotypically "feminine" style of communication, ethics, and interaction—emphasizing caring, concern with personal relationships, and egalitarianism.[170]

The very being of men and women is different, so of course how they interact with ministry is different. One telling aspect of how men and women clergy interact differently with their congregation, as noted by Finlay, is that men seem to be more hierarchical and women prove to be more personalized, more egalitarian, and more concerned with broader social justice issues.[171] These characteristics as observed by Finlay do not mean that this applies universally. I know some men who are very personalized, work hard to even the playing field in ministry, and do nothing but preach social justice; and I know women who do the inverse.

In thinking about the image of women in a congregation, it leads me to do my own critical reflection about how I view women in ministry and how I could extend my ministry in a way that would be more inclusive. Considering how society alone has sculpted my view about women, I see how those structures even play out within the church.

The groundbreaking work by Emilie Townes, *Womanist Ethics and the Cultural Production of Evil* (specifically chapter 2), helped me reflect more deeply on the view of women in ministry and the impact that it could have on their future role in ministry.

Townes starts off chapter 2 of her work by elucidating Toni Morrison's essay "The Site of Memory." Townes explains how several themes within that essay help introduce themes within the chapter: imagination, history, the fantastic, the power of images, and memory.[172] Townes uses Toni Morrison's experience as a writer of stories within the slave narrative category to center the argument between memory and history. Morrison views her writings as reaching beyond the level in which those who recorded slave narratives did—noting that the ones recording the narratives wrote to shield the audience from

---

170. Ibid., 7.
171. Ibid.
172. Emilie M. Townes, *Womanist Ethics and the Cultural Production of Evil* (New York: Palgrave Macmillan, 2007), 11.

parts of the truth that may have been less appealing to the consciousness of the White audience and, therefore, did not deal with the interior of the narratives.[173]

In her writing, Morrison presents a more concentrated narrative where the interior of the lives of the slaves were respected and honored, even the horror. Memory is important to this approach to the writing of slave narratives, but in cases where the recorder of the memory dismissed, skipped over, watered down, or downright did not write the fullness of what occurred, for whatever reason, Morrison relies upon imagination to construct the interior that has been left out, which she claims is more productive for her.[174]

Centering the chapter around Morrison's reasoning of writing and the wider societal misunderstanding of what she was attempting to do and write is a strength of this chapter. The disregard of the memories and the stories told to the recorder of the slave narrative, for whatever reason, is the foundation for Townes' subsequent scholarship in this chapter regarding identifying whose memory and whose history is of worth and value. How we value the worth of those memories and history therefore produces a culture of evil.

In looking at the history of my own denomination (National Baptist Convention, USA, Inc.), when it comes to telling and sharing history, we have a running list of men whom we call on and, sparingly, we speak of women. Looking toward the future of our convention and as a denomination overall, there must be a shift in our approach of how we speak of women, how we tell the history of women, and how we include women in the work that God has called us to do. Even in this, we as men within the convention should let women tell their own truths from their own perspectives and express their own spiritual revelations as children of God. Without doing this, I don't foresee a convention that is viable and thriving in the twenty-first century.

How Townes, in chapter 2, writes about memory and history showed me the need to advocate for this way of thinking. In my experience—and having lived it as a man who has a voice and power and privilege—I now can be an ally for my sister co-laborers in an attempt to further dismantle the "good-old-boy clubs."

---

173. Ibid.
174. Ibid., 12.

For Townes, both memory and history are "dance partners" that complement one another. She uses both within this chapter to show how they have been used to produce a culture of hegemony and evil within our society.[175] The construct of both memory and history, where the dominant culture determines what is written, remembered, and understood to be of other cultures without critique or analysis, supports the idea of inferiority of one group while it embraces and uplifts another group.

Therefore, I see Morrison writing within the interior lives of slaves because there was a culture present that saw parts of the truth within the stories as unneeded and was deliberately left out of history. The memories of the slave that did not fit into the "normative narrative" and were left out helped reshape history and contributed to a culture through memory and history of hegemony and oppression. This was done through the slave narratives by painting a picture of "darkies" and "porch monkeys" who were lazy and not telling horrendous parts, which produced a culture and image within this country as a depiction of Black people.

This has historically been how men of the church have dealt with women within the church as well—seeing our narratives as valuable and their experiences as invalid. Consider the history of the Christian church (which has undoubtedly influenced the Black church) and how we deal with women as well. Therefore, there is a responsibility of people with power to advance those who have no power; and the lack of doing so can find us as men in danger of judgment.

The future role of women in ministry cannot be spoken of outside of the power role of men and how we use our power to advance these works of justice, not only in the world but also within our churches. The prophet Amos gives a biblical explanation for the responsibility that we have as people of privilege. His explanation buttresses the point I am making about the need to use power and privilege to guarantee justice for women in the Gospel ministry.

Amos was an eighth-century prophet during the reign of King Jeroboam II of Israel (northern kingdom) and King Uzziah of Judah (southern kingdom) between the years of 793 and 753 BCE.[176] As I see

---
175. Ibid., 18.
176. Leander E. Keck, ed. *The New Interpreter's Bible: A Commentary in Twelve Volumes* (Nashville: Abingdon Press, 2003), 38.

and understand the text of Amos, there is a thesis and an antithesis in the words of Amos. The thesis is that God is calling God's children to works of justice, which Amos states throughout most of his writing. In the context of this work, it means men using power and privilege to advance women equally in the Gospel ministry. Amos uses rhetoric and the situation of the times to preach and prophesy about justice. Amos' antithesis is that God does not want followers of the cult at the expense of justice.

This in the context of the future role of women in ministry and men as an ally of change means that men cannot continue our normal way of doing things in ministry and think that God is pleased with our "whoop for entertainment" and not with our "help for edification." This means, in the context of this research, that there are pastors who have women as preachers to fill ceremonial roles but will not allow them to use the full depth of their gifts, because of tradition. These men are fulfilling ceremonious role of advocacy but not seeking to dismantle the structures of evil that Townes writes about to bring equality to the Gospel with women's equality. For Amos, God requires more of the Israelites than cultic sacrifices and ritualistic practices; God requires justice as well. This is true in regard to ministry also.

Amos lived in Tekoa, which was twelve miles south of Jerusalem. Tekoa was a small agrarian town during the time of Amos. He earned his living by raising sheep and taking care of sycamore trees. Tekoa economy was suffering because they had very limited resources and most of those resources were used to support the monarchy, the king's army, the courts of the land, and even the priests and prophets of the shrines.[177] Neither the priests nor the prophet said (or did) anything to relieve the economic woes of Tekoa and found ways to profit off the already hurting economy for themselves. This aligns with the "Black church" and women. While the poor were plenteous in Tekoa (see Amos 1), women were plenteous within the church, and the people in power (rich people in the text and men in the church) were doing little to advance God's order of justice.

Without a doubt Amos saw the suffering of the people of his land and was called of God to become a prophet. Amos would eventually leave the town of Tekoa. He preached to an assemblage of people (probably at

---

177. Ibid., 23.

Bethel) his message of justice.[178] He also went to Samaria (the capital of the northern kingdom) and preached.[179] The idea that Amos might have preached this message at Bethel, for me, justifies his critique of the cult. Being called of God as a prophet and going to Bethel, the house of God speaks to his convictions and confidence in this message and in God's approval, as I see it, of the message.

Amos' message came at a time of postwar prosperity in the middle of the eighth century. Amos began prophesying late during the reign of King Jeroboam II, who had ended a century-and-a-half war with Syria and brought prosperity to the northern kingdom.[180] Amos was in a world of happiness and yet he preached against the prosperity of God—blessing the people for their faithfulness to the cult—as not being the true nature of God.[181]

Not only was the northern kingdom prospering well under Jeroboam but also, the southern kingdom of Judah was prospering under Uzziah. With such prosperity, it seems as if an era of luxury had returned to both kingdoms as it was under Solomon.[182] This era of luxury was filled with prosperity of the people and of the land. The people assumed it was because of their cultic practices and sacrifices that they were being honored by God with earthly riches.[183] This way of thinking, for Amos, was not so. Amos was very critical of the cultic religion and stood in opposition of this way of thinking. While this was an offense against Israel, this was not the premise of the message that Amos was preaching.

Amos, throughout the book, addresses the sin of the people. Amos addressed the merchant class who could not wait until the Sabbath was over so they could continue to cheat the poor.[184] Amos addressed the wives of the rich who placed demands on their husbands, influencing them to "crush the needy."[185] Amos addressed those that had profited from the present structure of the society and were complacent and would not do anything to aid the poor.[186]

---

178. Billy K. Smith and Frank S. Page, *Amos, Obadiah, Jonah: An Exegetical and Theological Exposition of Holy Scripture NIV Text (The New American Commentary)* (Nashville, TN; Holman Reference, 1995), 61; Amos 2:6-16, 89.
179. *Interpreters Bible Commentary; New American Commentary*, 796; see Amos 3:9–4:3.
180. William J. Doorly, *Prophet of Justice: Understanding the Book of Amos* (Mahwah, New Jersey: Paulist Press, 1989), 39.
181. *Interpreters Bible Commentary*, 767.
182. Ibid., 769.
183. See Amos 4:4-13.
184. See Amos 8:4-6.
185. Amos 4:1 (NIV)
186. See Amos 6.

While Amos addressed the sins of the people, Amos also addressed those who had been victimized by the current structure of society. Amos identified the victimized as the poor, the needy, and the righteous in two places (see 2:6 and 5:12). These were the people who were suffering at the hands of the rich and well-to-do people. Amos says that the rich sell the righteous for silver and the needy for a pair of sandals.[187]

By this time in Israel, families had lost their land and the passing of the land down through the male line had been ignored.[188] Families were now working the land that their families once owned, and were now tenant farmers and were being charged high amounts of rent, being made to grow not what they needed to survive, but what Samaria needed for international trade.[189]

All of this leads us to the irresponsibility of Israel as it leads us to the irresponsibility of men regarding women in ministry. Amos was indignant with the vile atrocity of injustice and used his power to advance the cause of those who were oppressed. This for me is the mark of a prophet. Preaching against the tide of prosperity and filthy lucre and demanding that those with power and privilege use it for its God-given purpose—advancing God's kingdom on the earth and not the kingdom of this world—took great courage.

This is still the case today. There are some preachers and churches who have stood as Amos stood, and call women to high-ranking positions within their congregations and even as the pastor. Within the Black Baptist church the example is clear with the call of Rev. Dr. Eboni Marshall-Turman, who was the youngest woman appointed as Assistant Minister at The Abyssinian Baptist Church, City of New York, and being only the second woman to preside over the ordinances of the church in their almost 210-year history. In the spirit of Amos, The Hampton Ministers Conference, which is an ecumenical organization but has historically been aligned with the Black Baptist movement of Virginia, elected their first woman president, Rev. Dr. Suzan Johnson Cook, in 2002. Christ Missionary Baptist Church of Memphis, Tennessee, has had a woman at the helm of their church since 1995 with Rev. Dr. Gina Stewart. These three are examples from the Black Baptist tradition (whose legacy I am an inheritor of) who have aligned themselves with

---

187. See Amos 2:6.
188. Doorly, 24.
189. Ibid., 25.

Amos' call to advocating for people whose power has been snuffed out because of injustice.

The irresponsibility of men regarding advancing women in ministry led me back to Townes' work on the *Womanist Ethics and the Cultural Production of Evil*. Townes uses her words as a womanist writer and her intellect to sculpt a theory of the understanding of the minds of those that have historically oppressed people. By blending Michael Foucault's use of fantasy and imagination and Antonio Gramsci's understanding of hegemony in coining the term "fantastic hegemonic imagination," Townes teaches that the imagination, because of the way it functions, makes evil ordinary by holding structural evil firmly in its place and making it hard to dismantle.

Through history, memory, and imagination, we as a society embrace very negative stereotypes and make those stereotypes the norm by which we interact and respond to those who historically have been "othered" by the society in which we live. It is because of how we view history, memory, and imagination that beauty and sacredness of the Black female body and character has been marred and disfigured by the wider society as nothing more than a property to be used, abused, and misused by anyone and everyone. Townes writes, "[T]he fantastic hegemonic imagination uses a politicized sense of history and memory to create and shape its worldview. It sets in motion whirlwinds of images used in the cultural production of evil. The images have an enormous impact on how we understand the world, as well as others and ourselves in the world."[190]

Because our minds and our attitudes are accustomed (arguably numbed) to such stereotypes as the Welfare Queen, the Mammy figure, and Aunt Jemima, these figures can become in our minds nothing more than the reality of who and what the Black woman is, acts like, and should be. Conversely, some preachers' thoughts of women are that women are trying to "take a man's place," "usurping authority," and even "wanting to be a man."

The fantastic hegemonic imagination is real and is used in these ways (even in the twenty-first century) and many of us do not recognize or realize it. It is producing a culture of evil and disturbing caricatures of the Black woman, and men within the church can be seen at the forefront of this evil movement.

---

190. Townes, 21.

The Agency of Women

I do not want to focus this paper on the sole responsibility of men and negate the power that women have over their own bodies, their legacies, and the ministry that has been entrusted to them.

Women historically have been marginalized and oppressed. When they were children, they were the property of their fathers; when they were married, they became the property of their husbands. Life for women was restricted and limited to being subservient to men. Although women were under the control of men in their lives, some found ways to make themselves less marginalized. Women would fast more frequently to have control of their lives. They would forsake themselves of food, sex, and worldly wealth. Gluttony in their minds was a form of lust and fasting was a way to renounce the lust. Often, they would note that when Eve ate of the forbidden fruit, sin entered the world; and, with the Eucharist through Christ's death, salvation entered the world.

The future role of women within the church lies in men's using our power to advance them, which is important; but men's responsibility must coincide with allowing women the space to advocate for themselves, using their own voices and their own narratives to advance themselves. The faith of women, as exemplified by three women within the Christian narrative, shows how women can use their own power and agency to advance themselves in the world of hegemony they inherited.

St. Birgitta of Sweden and Lois and Eunice, the mother and grandmother of Timothy, show how their faith and their agency opened doors for them and left a legacy of good works and ministry in a patriarchal society.

St. Birgitta of Sweden was a woman of the Christian faith whose faith was counted unto her as righteousness. St. Birgitta was known for forsaking self and worldly pleasures. It is after the death of her husband that she began to take on the full regalia of suffering. Women of the thirteenth, fourteenth, and fifteenth centuries, especially, were known to do this. It is through this lens of suffering that her witness as a Christian woman gained notoriety and her story was preserved.

St. Birgitta, from a young age, wanted to be celibate and commit herself wholly to the Lord. She could not, because, at the age of twelve, she was made to marry her husband, by her father. (Again, we encounter a woman being told what to do by a man and not having authority over herself.)

In looking at a more inclusive ministry for women, there will have to be a shift in the way we do things. St. Birgitta could only control her body after her husband was dead. What does that say to or about her ministry of suffering before his death?

St. Birgitta was a woman who, in today's time, would be a part of an elite family. She gave all her possessions to her children and to the poor. She did this so she could follow God in poverty. Suffering is still a part of the Christian church. In suffering, one is thought to be closer to God. St. Birgitta wanted to live in simple conditions. That is why she gave all of her possessions away and why she wore old, ragged clothing. She forsook her body by fasting more than the required times. She would not sleep on a mattress when she did sleep. And she committed her days to prayer and service for the Lord. She took suffering literally and would perform self-mutilation by allowing candle wax to drip on her skin. Her commitment to her religion was noble. She left her home by God's command to travel to Rome, where she would sit with the poor at monasteries. St. Birgitta caused herself great suffering and affliction as part of her spiritual life. Hers was a life after which many should model their lives, and she would become a saint less than one hundred fifty years after her death.

In the opening lines of his second epistle to Timothy, Paul writes about Timothy's grandmother named Lois and his mother named Eunice who left a legacy of faith to their grandson and son. After opening the correspondence with a transitional Christian greeting, this older believer informed the younger leader of his gratefulness to the God of his ancestors and of his constant prayer for him. A part of this seasoned saint's recollection also included the younger minister's tears. The tears could have arisen as a result of the two men's parting company at some earlier date, or the tears could have resulted from the fact that the older saint had been imprisoned on account of his preaching the Gospel of Christ. Or still his tears could have occurred for some other unstated but understood reason. In any event, the older imprisoned apostle looked forward to seeing the young pastor in the future, an occasion that would fill him with joy.

In addition to remembering the young believer in prayer and recalling his tears and intensely longing to see him again, this writer also had a flashback. He walked down memory lane regarding this young man's grandmother Lois, and his mother, Eunice. He must have known them in the context of serving in the church, for he recalled their faith. The women were serving in a church where patriarchy was alive and well, yet their legacy was left on record because they refused to let their gender hinder ministry. It was the faith of these two women that made Paul consider Timothy "a chip off the old block!"

Eunice and Lois left Timothy a legacy of faith. What was the nature of this legacy? How might we characterize this faith? What by-product of the Spirit was there in Lois and Eunice, yet also found clear expression in the servant life of Timothy?

Further, it shows us how even though oppressed we can find glimmers of hope in advancing our cause through being faithful and at the same time fighting oppression within the system.

This legacy of faith that Lois and Eunice left Timothy is a transgender faith. By transgender I mean that it welcomed both males and females. Timothy's faith came through his grandmother Lois, and his mother, Eunice. Notice that his grandfathers and his father are conspicuously absent from his spiritual history. This suggests the ready inclusion of women in the composition, perpetuation, and operation of the early New Testament church. We know of Peter, James, John, and Paul, but several biblical observations support an integrationist claim.

At the circumcision and presentation of the eight-day-old Jesus in Jerusalem, Luke claims that a prophetess named Anna appeared and began to praise the child for redemption. Luke also informs his readers that as Jesus went through the cities and villages proclaiming the Good News of the kingdom of God, not only were the twelve male disciples there, but there were some women (Mary Magdalene, Joanna, Susanna, and many others) who provided for Jesus and His disciples out of their resources—out of that with which God had blessed them. There were also heads of households.

Also, we read of Mary and Martha of Bethany, two of Jesus' closest friends, along with their brother Lazarus, whom Jesus raised from the dead (see John 11). Mark, Matthew, and Luke all speak of women's witnessing the crucifixion of Jesus at a distance while John portrays them as being near the cross. All four canonical Gospels speak of women as the first persons to witness Jesus' empty tomb and to receive the word about His resurrection.

The evangelist known as John identifies Mary Magdalene as the first to see and converse with the risen Lord. I come to tell you that women along with men tarried together in the upper room in Jerusalem until the day of Pentecost when the Holy Spirit's windy and fiery invasion affected all who were there. In Acts 5:14, the narrator reports the rapid growth of the church and declares that *"more than ever believers were added to the Lord, great numbers of both men and women"* (NRSVUE). The Acts author further identifies a woman named Tabitha, whose Greek name was Dorcas, as a disciple devoted to good works and acts of charity. The apostle Paul recommended to the church of Rome a sister named Phoebe, whom he recognized as a minister or deacon of the church. Lydia, a dealer in purple cloth, received the Word of God through Paul at Philippi, where she and her entire household, that she apparently headed, were baptized. Priscilla was half of the wife-husband evangelistic team that willingly assisted the apostle Paul in his ministry endeavors and housed him for eighteen months as he preached in Corinth. Paul pushed the matter even further in his inclusion of women when he wrote a radical statement to the Galatians. He said there is neither Jew nor Greek, there is no longer slave or free, there is no longer male or female—for all of us are one in Christ Jesus.

For these and other reasons, we label this legacy of faith a transgender faith. This is no less the case in the African American legacy story. Not only men but also women have been responsible for forming this great heritage. I speak here of women like Sister Kelly, an ex-slave from Tennessee, who described her dramatic conversion experience at twelve years of age as a voice that said, "It's just in God's hands and you must praise and bless God all the time." I'm talking about women like the early nineteenth-century preacher Jarena Lee, who insisted that if a man may preach because the Savior died for him, why not the woman seeing that He died for her also? I refer here to women like abolitionist Maria Stewart who, in September 1832 at Boston's Franklin Hall, challenged the men there, saying, "Have the sons of Africa no souls? Feel they no ambitious desire?" I lift up women like Amanda Berry Smith, the traveling evangelist with a worldwide reputation; Sojourner Truth, the great spokesperson for the abolition of slavery; Harriet Tubman, the fearless liberator of more than three hundred slaves; Katherine Harris, who, in 1850, housed and cared for escaped slaves in her home. What about Rosa Young, the educator who started a school for the least of these in Rosebud, Alabama, in

1912? Or S. Mattie Fisher, who conducted a community survey out of Chicago's Olivet Baptist Church in 1918 to aid the residents? Or what about Nannie Helen Burroughs, the great pioneer of Black Baptist women and one of the principal founders of the National Baptist Women's Convention in 1900? And surely we must mention the civil rights heroines Fannie Lou Hamer, Rosa Parks, Joann Robinson, Coretta Scott King, Ella Baker, Septima Clark, Bernice Johnson, Lydia Bryan Hall, and Jerdine Williams. They were all women of force, women of fortitude, women of freedom, and women of faith. The African American legacy of faith includes not only great men of faith but also great women of faith. It is not a matter of either/or, it is rather a case of both-and.

Our forebears presented us with a transgender faith, one that includes women who, just as their male counterparts, heard the call, accepted the job, met the challenge, and performed the deed. These women made the grade, bore the burden, carried the load, delivered the goods. These women endured the pain, followed the path, gave the offering, held the line, inspired the masses, led the charge, managed the work, opened the door, prayed the prayers, preached the sermons, and found the lost. These women came through just like the men did.

In the end, we must realize that we are God's handiwork, created in Christ Jesus to do good work (see Ephesians 2:10). If we are to become the true ecclesia—that is, the called-out body of Christ living and breathing in this world—we must live in the Spirit to move us toward a ministry that is welcoming of all of God's creation. In the words of Joseph Cook,

> *Hand in hand, man and woman build the home; hand in hand they ought to build the state and the church. Hand in hand they left an earthly Paradise Lost; hand in hand they are likely to enter, if at all, an earthly Paradise Regained.*[191]

---

191. Willard, 14.

Chapter 5

Bridging the Gap between Legacy and Destiny (Conclusion)

In *Breaking the Stained-glass Ceiling*, I set out to tell the truth about our legacy—to share the stories, lift the voices, and affirm the witness of women whose faith and leadership have shaped the Black church. I have profiled leaders across denominational lines, honored the pioneers who paved the way, and celebrated those faithfully serving today.

I believe, without hesitation or apology, that the church cannot thrive without fully embracing the leadership and spiritual gifts of women. For the Lord has poured out His Spirit *"on all flesh"* (Joel 2:28a, NRSVUE). From the earliest days until now, Black women have been central to the church's growth—proclaiming the Word (see Acts 2:17-18), guiding ministries (see Romans 16:1-2), organizing communities (see Titus 2:3-5), and sustaining kingdom work through prayer, vision, and action (see Luke 18:1). Their impact is undeniable, yet far too often, their leadership has been overlooked. Their contributions have gone unrecognized, yet they deserve the honor they are due.

Affirming women in ministry by embracing their calling and giftedness, and giving them a rightful place to serve, is not the end of the story; it is part of the larger vision I hold as President of the National Baptist Convention, USA, Inc. My heart is not for a position; it is for the people: pastors laboring in the vineyard (see 1 Corinthians 15:58), congregations serving our communities, and the next generation of leaders waiting to be empowered. The Convention, founded on mission and evangelism, must make those principles not only visible but also prevailing. Our Convention is aging, and we must intentionally prepare to pass the baton—rooted in mission, driven by evangelism, strengthened by education, and committed to justice.

In 1977, I joined the Convention under the late Rev. Dr. Joseph Harrison Jackson, our twelfth president. Dr. Jackson was a Baptist preacher par excellence—a visionary pastor, political activist, denominational leader, husband, and father—renowned for his unmatched skill in homiletics. His leadership at Olivet Baptist Church in Chicago, Illinois, remains the longest continuous pastorate in its history. Dr. Jackson sought to educate and equip African Americans to sustain their institutions, build robust economic structures, and achieve self-sufficiency—free from dependency on external systems. His vision of empowerment, discipline, and dignity has profoundly shaped my own leadership philosophy. During Dr. Jackson's presidency, I observed the landscape and dynamics of the Convention without being directly involved in its internal operations. It was a season to watch and learn before being given any visibility.

As a young pastor of Jeffries Cross Baptist Church in Burlington, North Carolina, desiring change, I cast my vote for Dr. T. J. Jemison, who was elected in 1982 in Miami, Florida, as the Convention's thirteenth president. In January 1984, I met Dr. W. Franklyn Richardson, General Secretary in the Jemison presidential administration, who invited me to the platform as a young preacher. Through Dr. Richardson's mentorship and Dr. Jemison's leadership, I was given opportunities for leadership development, visibility, and engagement in the inner workings of the Convention. It became for me a classroom without walls—a place where I began to learn the work of building a legacy.

I have now served in this Convention faithfully for more than forty-five years, working under six additional presidents since those early days. From each of them, I gleaned lessons in leadership and mentorship that have shaped me for such a time as this. Just as Dr. Jackson prepared his generation, I am committed to equipping the next with the tools, knowledge, and faith needed not just to survive—but to thrive. My charge to the next generation is clear: build boldly, lead faithfully, and serve selflessly—so that this Convention will continue to stand as a beacon of strength, unity, and Gospel witness for generations yet to come.

When I first began this writing in 2018, our Convention told a different story. Women in ministry were too often unseen, unacknowledged, and certainly not affirmed within the Convention family. But thanks be to God that seven years later, by His grace, progress has been made, yet the work is not finished. Therefore, my visionary and strategic goals for our Convention are rooted in a prophetic call for relevance and vitality in the twenty-first century—a call that demands we honor every gift, embrace every servant of God, and maximize our collective impact in advancing the kingdom of God. These goals are the work of bridging the gap between legacy and destiny—honoring the faith of those who came before us while pressing forward into the future that God is calling us to build:

1. Unify all affiliated churches, auxiliaries, and entities—including the Sunday School Publishing Board and American Baptist College—under a shared mission, a coordinated vision, and a spirit of mutual accountability. Break down silos, strengthen collaboration, and ensure that every arm of our Convention moves in harmony toward kingdom impact.

2. Strengthen shared governance and operational efficiency to steward God's human, material, and financial resources with excellence and transparency—ensuring sustainability, increasing our capacity to serve, and expanding inclusion by fully engaging women in Convention leadership as equal partners in shaping the future of our work.

3. Prioritize Christian education as the foundation of our Convention to ensure spiritual growth and maturity, equipping the saints to edify the body of Christ and engage the world with biblical clarity and conviction.

4. Generate revenue beyond registration and sponsorships by pursuing strategic investments, entrepreneurial ventures, and partnerships that create long-term streams of income to fund ministry and missions.

5. Restore the Baptist World Center, our headquarters in Nashville, Tennessee, so that it may once again serve as a hub for the Convention's leadership and operations—fully utilizing its facilities for meetings, conferences, lectures, symposia, and ceremonies—while preserving its sacred ground as a living legacy of former President Jemison, Dr. Mary O. Ross, former President of the Women's Convention (Auxiliary), and Cecilia Nabrit Adkins, former Executive Director of the Sunday School Publishing Board. Dr. Ross and Dr. Adkins attended and participated in the dedication of Nashville's Baptist World Center on June 21, 1985, joining countless others who helped build the foundation upon which we now stand. May this sacred place remain a living monument to their vision, faith, and enduring legacy.

6. Build stronger relationships with young adults to ensure a seamless transition of leadership, preserve the vitality of the Convention, and secure the future of our mission.

7. Confront the pressing issues of our time, including but not limited to economics, crime, prison reentry, and racial injustice, by advancing criminal justice reform, economic empowerment, educational access, and social justice advocacy that dismantles systemic inequality.

8. Partner with the National Newspaper Publishers Association (NNPA), also known as The Black Press of America; the Coalition of Denominational Leaders; the National Association of Real Estate Brokers; the Gamaliel National Network; Elev8 Health, Inc., World Vision; FEMA; and the Red Cross to raise awareness of social justice issues impacting our communities, promote disaster readiness, expand home missions, and engage in a national listening initiative to unify and strengthen our churches.

9. Expand our global footprint with foreign missions—particularly in Africa—to strengthen bonds with our brothers and sisters on the continent, engage in shared ministry, and stand in solidarity as part of the global body of Christ.

Finally, I see a day when the stained-glass ceiling is not merely cracked and broken but shattered in all our churches. I see a day when every pulpit resounds with the voice of the called—man and woman, young and old. I see a day when the church rises in unity—standing on the Word, walking in the Spirit, and working in the kingdom. And when we dare to bridge that gap, vision turns into reality. Therefore, I call on every delegate, every pastor, every believer, to join in this movement. Let us take our Convention to higher heights, meet the urgent needs of our world, and declare with one voice that the Gospel is still Good News! We need all hands on deck. We need every voice proclaiming Christ until He comes again. And on that day, we shall lift one voice . . . one song . . . one praise—declaring to every nation and to every generation, with every tongue: To God be the glory for the great things He has done! To God be the glory for the great things He is doing! To God be the glory for the great things He will do!

Works Cited

African American Registry. *Barbara Harris, A Spiritual First.* June 12, 2000. http://www.aaregistry.org/historic_events/view/barbara-harris-spiritual-first (accessed February 20, 2017).

African Methodist Episcopal Church. *Tenth Episcopal District of the African Methodist Episcopal Church.* n.d. http://www.10thdistrictame.org/bishop.html (accessed February 20, 2017).

Allen, Bob. "The 'Billy Graham Rule' and Women in Ministry." *Baptist News Global,* 6 April 2017: 1.

Andrews, William L., editor. *Sisters of the Spirit: Three Black Women's Autobiographies of the Nineteenth Century.* Bloomington: Indiana University Press, 1986.

Archives of the Episcopal Church, The. "The Right Reverend Barbara Harris." 2008. https://exhibits.episcopalarchives.org/s/episcopal-church-women/page/barbara-harris (accessed February 20, 2017).

Baker-Fletcher, Karen. "Voice, Vision and Spirit: Black Women Preaching in the Nineteenth Century" in *Sisters Struggling in the Spirit: A Women of Color Theological Anthology.* Louisville, Kentucky: Women's Ministries Program Area, National Ministries Division, and Christian Faith and Life Program Area, Congregational Ministries Division, Presbyterian Church (U.S.A.), 1994.

Best, Wallace. "The Spirit of the Holy Ghost is a Male Spirit: African American Preaching Women and the Paradoxes of Gender" in *Women and Religion in the African Diaspora. Knowledge, Power and Performance;* R. Marie Griffith and Barbara Dianne Savage, editors. Baltimore: Hopkins University Press, 2006.

Blackpast.org.

Blassingame, John W. *The Slave Community: Plantation Life in the Antebellum South.* New York: Oxford University Press, 1979.

Cantarow, Ellen. "Portrait of Prathia Hall." Medium.com. January 3, 2017. https://medium.com/@ellencantarow/ii-portrait-of-prathia-hall-63fed124049c (accessed February 20, 2017).

Chandler, D. L. "Little Known Black History Fact: Prathia Hall." black americaweb.com. n.d. https://Blackamericaweb.com/2016/06/15/little-known-Black-history-fact-prathia-hall/ (accessed March 1, 2017).

Doorly, William J. *Prophet of Justice: Understanding the Book of Amos.* Mahwah, New Jersey: Paulist Press, 1989.

Emmert, Ashley. "The State of Female Pastors." Women Leaders. October 15, 2015. https://www.christianitytoday.com/women-leaders/2015/october/state-of-female-pastors.html.

Fiedler, Maureen, editor. *Breaking Through the Stained Glass Ceiling: Women Religious Leaders in Their Own Words.* New York: Seabury Books, 2010.

Finlay, Barbara. *Facing the Stained Glass Ceiling: Gender in a Protestant Seminary.* Maryland: University Press of America, 2002.

Fitts, Leroy. *A History of Black Baptists.* Nashville, TN: Broadman Press, 1985.

Foster, Richard J. *Celebration of Discipline: The Path to Spiritual Growth.* New York: HarperCollins, 2018; first published 1978.

Gilkes, Cheryl T. *If It Wasn't for the Women . . .: Black Women's Experience and Womanist Culture in Church and Community.* New York: Orbis Books, 2000.

Grant, Jacqueline. "Womanist Theology: Black Women's Experience as a Source for Doing Theology," in *Sisters Struggling in the Spirit.* Lewis, N. B., et al. Louisville: Presbyterian Church, 1994.

Grenz, Stanley J., and Denise Muir Kjesbo. *Women in the Church: A Biblical Theology of Women in Ministry.* Lisle, Illinois: InterVarsity Press, 1995.

Griffith, R. Marie, and Barbara Dianne Savage, editors. *Women and Religion in the African Diaspora: Knowledge, Power, and Performance.* Baltimore, Maryland: John Hopkins University Press, 2006.

Hall, Prathia. "When Faith Trembles." February 6, 2000. http://www.30goodminutes.org/index.php/archives/23-member-archives/648-prathia-hall-program-4318 (accessed February 20, 2017).

Hooks, Bell. *Feminist Theory: From Margin to Center.* Boston: South End Press, 1984.

Hopkins, Dwight. *Down, Up, and Over: Slave Religion and Black Theology.* Minneapolis, Minnesota: Fortress Press, 2000.

Johnson, James Weldon. *God's Trombones: Seven Negro Sermons in Verse.* New York: Penguin Classics, 1976.

Jones, Martha. "Make Us a Power," in *Women and Religion in the African Diaspora: Knowledge, Power, and Performance;* R. Marie Griffith and Barbara Dianne Savage, editors. Baltimore: John Hopkins University Press, 2006.

Keck, Leander E., ed. *The New Interpreter's Bible: A Commentary in Twelve Volumes.* Nashville: Abingdon Press, 2003.

Kindig, Jessie. "Bloody Sunday Protest March, Selma, Alabama, March 7, 1965." Blackpast.org. November 24, 2007. http://www.Blackpast.org/aah/bloody-sunday-selma-alabama-march-7-1965 (accessed February 20, 2017).

Lamb, Yvonne S. *My Soul Rhythms: Prayer Stories to Ignite Your Spirit.* Nashville, TN: WestBow Press, 2015.

———. "Prathia Hall: A Barrier-Breaking Woman Preacher." Good Faith Media. March 28, 2011. http://www.ethicsdaily.com/prathia-hall-a-barrier-breaking-woman-preacher-cms-17660 (accessed March 1, 2017).

LaRue, Cleophus. *The Heart of Black Preaching.* Louisville, KY: Westminster John Knox Press, 1999.

Lee, Jarena. *Religious Experience and Journal of Mrs. Jarena Lee, Giving an Account of Her Call to Preach the Gospel.* (First published in Philadelphia in 1836. Lastly published by CreateSpace Independent Publishing Platform, 2017).

Lincoln, C. Eric, and Lawrence Mamiya. *The Black Church in the African American Experience.* Durham, NC: Duke University Press, 1990.

McKenzie, Vashti M. *Not Without a Struggle: Leadership Development for African American Women in Ministry—Revised and Updated.* Cleveland, Ohio: Pilgrim Press, 2012.

McMickle, M. *An Encyclopedia of African American Christian Heritage.* Philadelphia: Judson Press, 2002.

Mitchell, Ella Pearson. *Women: To Preach or Not to Preach: 21 Outstanding Black Preachers Say Yes!* Valley Forge, Pennsylvania: Judson Press, 1991.

Mitchell, Henry H. *Black Preaching.* New York: Harper & Row, 1979.

———. *Black Preaching: The Recovery of a Powerful Art.* Nashville, TN: Abingdon Press, 1990.

PBS. "PEOPLE OF FAITH: Prathia Hall." *This Far by Faith* (Episode 4). 2003. http://www.pbs.org/thisfarbyfaith/people/prathia_hall.html (accessed March 1, 2017).

Smith, Billy K., and Frank S. Page. *Amos, Obadiah, Jonah: An Exegetical and Theological Exposition of Holy Scripture NIV Text (The New American Commentary)*. Nashville, TN; Holman Reference, 1995.

SNCC Legacy Project. "Prathia Hall." Duke University. n.d. https://snccdigital.org/people/prathia-hall/ (accessed March 1, 2017).

The HistoryMakers. "Bishop Barbara Harris." February 12, 2007. http://www.thehistorymakers.com/biography/bishop-barbara-harris (accessed February 20, 2017).

Thurman, Howard. *Disciplines of the Spirit*. New York: Harper & Row, 1963.

Townes, Emilie M. *Womanist Ethics and the Cultural Production of Evil*. New York: Palgrave Macmillan, 2007.

Tucker, Melanie. "Hines elected first female bishop for AME Zion Church." *The Daily Times*, September 10, 2012.

Turman, Eboni Marshall. *Toward a Womanist Ethic of Incarnation: Black Bodies, the Black Church, and the Council of Chalcedon*. New York: Palgrave Macmillan, 2013.

Virtue, David. "The Legacy of Barbara Harris." Virtue Online. March 4, 2009. http://www.virtueonline.org/legacy-barbara-harris-if-aholes-had-wings-lambeth-1998 (accessed February 20, 2017).

Virtue, David, and Michael Heidt. "Episcopal Bishop Barbara Harris Denies Sacrament of Marriage." Catholic Online. July 16, 2009. http://www.catholic.org/news/national/story.php?id=34090 (accessed February 20, 2017).

Whelchel, Love Henry. *Hell Without Fire: Conversion in Slave Religion*. Nashville, TN: Abingdon Press, 2002.

Wikipedia. https://en.wikipedia.org/wiki/Barbara_Harris_(bishop).

Willard, Frances Elizabeth. *Woman in the Pulpit*. Boston: D. Lothrop Co., 1888.

Wilson, Teisha. "Jarena Lee (1783–185?)." Blackpast.org. January 19, 2007. http://www.Blackpast.org/aah/lee-jarena-1783 (accessed January 2017).

Dr. Boise Kimber

Dr. Boise Kimber was elected the nineteenth president of the National Baptist Convention, USA, Inc.—the country's largest African American denomination—on September 5, 2024. A visionary leader who seamlessly combines faith and activism, President Kimber is transforming denominational structures to promote greater inclusivity and opportunity for all.

As president of the National Baptist Convention, Dr. Kimber focuses on strengthening the denomination's infrastructure, advancing social justice rooted in the Gospel, building bridges across generations, expanding economic empowerment, and revitalizing spiritual vitality in churches nationwide.

As pastor of First Calvary Baptist Church in New Haven and New Hope Baptist Church in Bridgeport, Connecticut, Dr. Kimber has committed his ministry to uplifting marginalized communities and tackling systemic challenges with conviction and purpose. His leadership extends beyond the pulpit, as he tirelessly works to create pathways for justice, equality, and opportunity across the country.

Dr. Kimber's dedication to elevating women's leadership within the Black church is more than words—it is a transformative effort. Under his leadership, women have been appointed to historic positions of authority, including Rev. Dr. Debbie Strickling-Bullock's groundbreaking appointment as chair of the Board of Directors of the Sunday School Publishing Board, one of the largest African American-owned publishing companies in the nation. These appointments reflect President Kimber's vision "to have women become a part of the administrative parts of our convention," signaling a new era for the denomination.

A dedicated scholar and theological leader, Dr. Kimber holds a Doctor of Ministry degree from United Theological Seminary, a Master of Sacred Theology degree from Yale Divinity School, a Master of Religious Education degree from Hartford Seminary, and a Bachelor of Arts degree in Sociology from Johnson C. Smith University. His rigorous academic background shapes his intellectual depth and commitment to holistic ministry that engages both spiritual and social aspects of faith.

Dr. Kimber is married to Reverend Shevalle T. Kimber, co-pastor of First Calvary Baptist Church, and together they are proud parents and grandparents. Their partnership in ministry and life embodies the inclusive leadership model that Dr. Kimber champions for the future of the Black church.

www.ingramcontent.com/pod-product-compliance
Lightning Source LLC
Chambersburg PA
CBHW050733010526
44107CB00010B/839